sweet
dreams

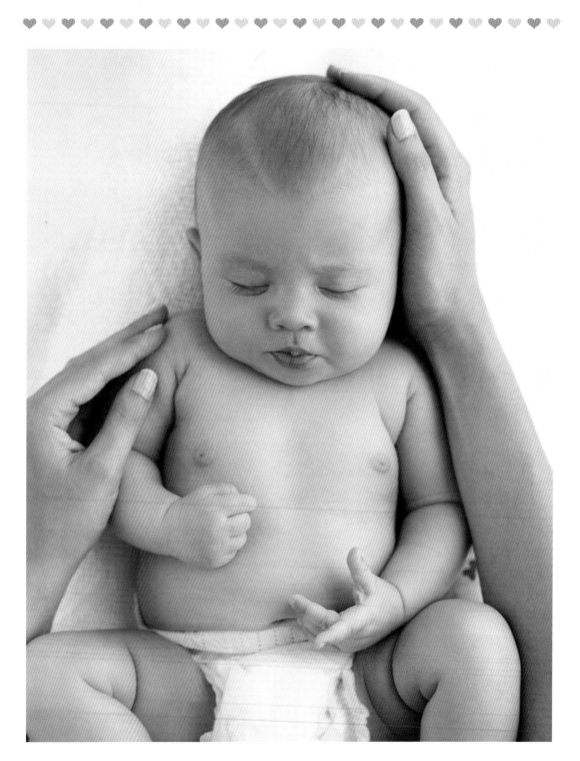

sweet
dreams

How to establish and maintain good sleep habits for your baby

ARNA SKULA

CARROLL & BROWN PUBLISHERS LIMITED

♥ Contents

First published in 2012 in
the United Kingdom by

Carroll & Brown Publishers Limited
20 Lonsdale Road
London NW6 6RD

Managing Art Editor Emily Cook
Editor Anne Yelland
Photography Jules Selmes
Translation from Icelandic Ian Watson

Text copyright © Arna Skúladóttir 2006
Compilation copyright
© Carroll & Brown Limited 2012

A CIP catalogue record for this book
is available from the British Library.

ISBN 978 907952 10 4
10 9 8 7 6 5 4 3 2 1

Reproduced by RALI, Spain
Printed and bound in China

Introduction

In this book, I explain what you can reasonably expect of your baby and the various ways that you can help him to sleep well and feel happy. Sleep is not an isolated phenomenon, but rather it is connected to many other things in a baby's life, and for this reason I also touch on subjects such as development, feeding, personality, individual rhythms, family life, outside circumstances and general wellbeing. Just after learning to stand, for example, a baby who has always slept well might start to wake up more often

Sleep and wake cycle charts

A feature of this book are the specially designed charts in chapter 4 showing sleep and wake times at different ages. On these charts, sleep times are shown in white, wake times in blue. The hours shown in the outside ring exist solely for purposes of illustration; they are not a prescription for what your baby should do. The inner numbers, which show the length of each sleeping or waking period in hours and minutes (1:30 or one hour 30 minutes) are the ones that matter.

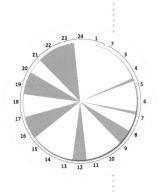

If you want to create a series of charts to see how your baby is sleeping and whether he is getting the number of hours he needs, make sure the sleep and wake times fall into the appropriate hours of the day and night for your family. Some pre-drawn charts to photocopy and fill in can be found on page 143.

at night and to have more difficulty falling asleep. Or, a baby
who has just got over a cold or the flu might keep on waking
up more often at night even though he is well again. Many
babies also start waking up at night more frequently after
their families move house or after the arrival of new siblings.
These are only a few examples of the connection between
sleep and the rest of your baby's life. I will highlight other
important factors as they come up in the book.

♥ Parental matters

When you are taking care of a baby, the most important thing to bear in mind is that each baby is born with a unique personality and temperament. Therefore, no single way of bringing up a baby will work for every child. This also applies to helping a baby to sleep; one baby, for example, might need help sticking to a routine, while another will need help accepting variation in a routine. Moreover, parents hold differing ideas about raising babies and society, too, has an impact on babycare. Whether a baby should be allowed to sleep in his parents' bed, or how strict the rules about bedtime should be are just two examples of contentious subjects. Although you may have strong opinions on a particular subject (you can't imagine 'refusing' your baby your bed, for example), you need to be flexible if you want to do what may be the best for your baby.

What babies need

Though apparently helpless when born, your baby is already an individual, and you will need time to get to know him. Similarly, your baby needs time to learn what you are like. Certainly, not all parents are alike. You may have waited for a baby for a very long time, or perhaps you would have gladly waited longer. You may feel quietly confident about taking care of your baby or anxious about the tremendous sense of responsibility that accompanies a baby's arrival. Perhaps it hasn't been long since you took full responsibility for your own life – and now you are supposed to feel capable of taking care of someone else's. You may have come from a large family and are knowledgeable about taking care of little ones or you may be an only child with very little experience of caring for babies. We all want to be good parents but we aren't completely sure what that means.

The two most important things in bringing up a child are to give him love and security and these two strands should always be woven together. If you give your child security without love, he may turn out calm and well-behaved but unhappy, and if you provide love without security, your child may be cheerful, but unruly and unsure of his own identity.

As with so many other aspects of growing up, however, different children need different amounts of love and security. Some children need a lot of what I call communication security, that is, being cared for consistently by the same people, but can tolerate much less of what I call environmental security, which is feeling secure in their physical surroundings. Other children need love above all and don't mind insecurity in their physical environment (they might, for example, be able to move house ten times in a short while without it having any effect).

In any event, it always works well to combine love and security, as for example, by setting limits (or rules) for a child out of affection. It's good to blend love and security together in the same gesture, by touching a child and saying gently but firmly "No, that's not allowed", for example. Teaching a baby good sleep habits often means setting limits.

Expressing love

You can say it with your eyes, with touch and in words.

♥

You can show it through your interest in your child's activities, and by being a good observer and admirer.

♥

You can teach it by enjoying quiet moments with your child.

LOVE

Love means, among other things, taking part in another person's life. It isn't enough just to feel fond of your baby; you need to say that you do and you need to let your baby feel that you do. It never stops being crucial for a baby's wellbeing to know that someone loves him. Your baby needs to know that you love him, even while you set limits for him. He needs to know that he is a part of a family, which is made up of him and you (and perhaps others, too). You need to show interest in his activities, and real interest in his life and preoccupations – even if it just means your watching the rain slide down a window together or playing with blocks side by side. That said, it is also important that your interest doesn't disturb your baby; don't take a toy or other object that he's playing with out of his hands. Instead, you need to remain an onlooker and admirer.

"It always works well to combine love and security, as for example, by setting limits (or rules) for a child out of affection."

SECURITY

A baby's feelings of security depend on two factors: his physical environment and his communication with people.

Environmental security

This means a baby feeling secure and at peace because he knows where his home is and where in the home he sleeps and eats. He also needs to know where he will be cared for during the day. As your baby grows older, he will, as well, want to keep his things in a particular place. If he needs to sleep somewhere other than at home, your baby will like to be surrounded by things that he normally has when going to sleep, like his comfort object – a blanket, favourite stuffed animal or dummy. Such objects keep his sense of security as undisturbed as possible.

Helping your baby

As each baby is different, the approach you take in managing sleep should depend on your child's temperament and personality. Here are two examples.

Lively and enterprising babies

Babies who are outgoing and explorative often need help sticking to a routine.

If your baby fits this category, it's important that you keep his sleep times and habits ordered and disciplined. If he is 'allowed to call the shots', he will want to sleep at very irregular times, which can really interfere with his ability to get a good night's sleep (as well as that of other family members).

Communication security

This involves a baby's need to rely on the same people caring for him from one day to the next, rather than one carer today and another tomorrow. A young baby should have only a few carers. As he gets older, however, he will find it beneficial to have contact with more people. Being exposed to a wider group of people gets him used to interacting with others and helps him build up an image of himself as an independent individual.

Communication security also depends on how parents respond to their baby's actions. If a baby sees that these responses are haphazard, for example, if he is allowed to sleep in the parental bed one night but is forbidden it another night or if his parents are willing to sit beside his bed while he is falling asleep one night but do not do so on another night, a baby starts feeling insecure. Capriciousness on the part of parents or other carers creates insecurity.

Sensitive-to-change babies

Babies who become upset and anxious in unfamiliar circumstances or surroundings need help accepting variation in a routine. These babies must get used to the fact that unexpected things happen, and that routines are liable to change.

If your baby is sensitive, you need to show him that daily life is full of minor variations, and that a little variation doesn't mean his whole world is turning upside down. For example, if your baby normally sleeps in a cot in his own room at home, he might need to learn to be happy napping in his carrycot in different surroundings now and again.

Some babies have a lot of trouble with changes to their daily routine, regardless of how small they are. The most successful approach is to train these babies calmly and slowly to accept variation and not demand too much too quickly.

Your baby needs to know what is allowed and what is not, and you need to give your baby secure and definite messages. If you do this, your baby will learn to trust you and to take you seriously.

You also need to show fairness in setting limits for your baby. Your baby doesn't always need to be happy with the rules, but he needs to know what to expect. Moreover, you need to know what you can reasonably expect of your baby so that you can make realistic demands of him. You cannot expect that your three-month-old baby will sleep all night without being fed, for example.

But what is fair and reasonable, and what is practical? The answer depends on the age and character of your baby and your baby's life circumstances. The age-specific chapter 4 (pages 70–131) discusses what, in practice, you can expect of your baby in terms of sleep and sleeping habits.

Security is

In the environment: Babies know where their home is, where they sleep, where they eat and where they spend the day.

♥

In communication: Babies know what is asked and required of them and what they can expect.

Upbringing – a team effort

A child's upbringing depends on both the child and his carer(s). You, the adult, need to be aware that you have to be the team manager. You also need to keep in mind that your child is far from a passive player; his reactions and personality have a real influence on the way things go. But children join 'the team' on different terms from adults. Your child lacks the maturity to worry about how you feel or what kind of influence your interaction with him has on you.

Take as an example, the decision to stop giving your one-year-old baby a bottle at night. He will probably cry for his bottle and won't be comforted. As a parent, you may think: "He's going to wake up his brother who is sleeping in the next room," or "Oh no, the neighbours are going to start complaining," or "I'm worried this will make him insecure," or "Poor thing, he is so hungry that I just better give him something small," or "Now he's going to wake up his father, who has to work a 12-hour day tomorrow," or "I'm going to be totally exhausted tomorrow, how am I supposed to be able to do all the things I need to do, when I haven't slept a wink. Why is it always me who gets up to see to him? His dad is snoring away as if nothing was happening. Argh."

You can see that the simple act of discontinuing a baby's night-time bottle doesn't just mean less sleep for one parent. It sets off a chain of worries and speculation about what effect the decision might have on the baby and on others in the family.

Your baby, however, just thinks, "I want a bottle; what on earth is going on here? I have a right to a bottle, that's how it's always been. I want a bottle NOW." He doesn't think "Goodness, how hard this must be for Mummy," or "I think I've woken up the whole house," or "It's not good for me to drink half a litre of milk at night, so I'm going to stop now." If your baby is the determined and tenacious type, he may not concede cheerfully.

PARENT-CHILD RELATIONSHIPS

Different factors have an impact on how parents and babies interact. An individual characteristic, such as temperament, is one of them. People are truly different. Some are excitable and easily stirred up, others like to follow rules precisely, and yet others dislike feeling that their lives are constrained.

Your general wellbeing, including fatigue due to chronically disturbed sleep, also has an influence on how you react to your baby. (The phrase 'Put on your own oxygen mask first and then assist your

> "The interactions that a baby has with those closest to him are thought to lay the foundation for his emotional development later on in life."

child' is used in air travel to point out that parents should take care of themselves so that they are better able to care for their children.) Constant fatigue can, for example, mean that you start to attend to your baby very quickly when he wakes up at night. You don't want him to wake up fully because you think that then it might become even harder to get him to fall asleep again. So you begin to do more for him than is really necessary. This could mean that your baby will want even more, even faster, service the following night.

Chronic parental sleeplessness can also lead to various kinds of anxiety; you might start to worry about issues that hadn't caused concern before. And there are other things – problems at work, family illnesses, financial worries, and much more – that can affect how you take care of your baby.

The interaction between a baby and his carer(s) lays the foundation for his later emotional development. Although your baby will not have any recollection of these times later on, your healthy interaction will promote the development of his mind and body. This means talking with him, involving him in things, giving him warmth and a reasonable amount of stimulation, but also respecting his wishes when he prefers peace and quiet.

MATTERS OF CHOICE

You need to do a little thinking and make some decisions about what expectations you have of your baby's sleeping patterns, and whether those expectations are realistic. It's never good to give a baby unclear messages. Most babies – at least those who sleep well – tolerate one-off exceptions, such as a single night when they have a little trouble going to sleep or wake up more often than usual to feed. But aside from occasional exceptions, babies' sleeping habits ought to be regular. In particular, if you are trying to change your baby's habits or correct sleep problems, you need to be very firm about what is and isn't allowed. You need to keep up this firmness for a few weeks at least. Depending on your attitude to certain situations – for example, whether he is welcome in the parental bed (see opposite) – your baby may need very clear messages. You may, for instance, find it necessary to completely stop letting your baby into your bed during both the day and at night – in other words, a total ban on using the bed at all including for nappy changes.

It's a good idea to think about the easiest way for a baby to learn what he needs to be taught. If, for example, the goal is to stop breastfeeding your baby at night, then it will be good to stop feeding him in bed as not doing so makes it harder for him to learn to stop feeding at night. Moreover, it is a good idea to stop breastfeeding in the bedroom entirely; in other words, you should shift all breastfeeding to another place. In short, you need to send your baby exceptionally clear messages and you must try to understand how he experiences everything that happens around him.

Sleeping in the parental bed

Many parents ask whether it is bad for their baby to sleep in their bed. Even more parents wish that those of us who work as sleep counsellors would take a clear and decisive position on the issue. But it's not such a simple matter, and most likely the right answer to the question is that it is up to the parents. Before choosing, though, you need to consider certain factors. You need to keep in mind that having your baby in your bed increases the risk of accidents. A baby can roll over unexpectedly and fall out of bed.

It's also important to get your baby used to the idea of sleeping in a place that belongs to him, in his own little 'nest'. If you let a baby sleep in your bed, then you need to be prepared to let him regard your bed as his own. We all need a regular place to sleep; it creates a sense of tranquillity and security. It's not good to be a night-time vagabond, sometimes sleeping on the sofa, sometimes in the living room, sometimes in this bed and sometimes in that one. There is a link between irregular sleep locations and sleep problems, but no strong links between sleep problems and babies sleeping in their parents' bed. The most common reason why parents let babies sleep in their bed is that they expect it will make caring easier. They do it when they are tired of having to get up out of bed again and again to deal with their baby. Overall, parents who choose to let their baby sleep in their bed just need to be on guard against accidents, and to be able to look at their bed as belonging to the whole family.

For many, it can be appealing that the parents' bed belongs to the whole family after five or six in the morning. It feels cosy when kids crawl up to you and snuggle for a little while before everyone gets up for the day. Some babies take to this approach well, but unfortunately it does not work for all of them.

Your baby's temperament can affect whether letting him into your bed works well or not. In general, co-sleeping works best with babies who are easy, calm and tractable.

Babies who are very active and energetic during the day often move around in their sleep as well (probably they are dreaming about what they did during the day). They journey to all corners of the bed, and give those who try to share it little peace. Babies like this also tend to wake up when the person sleeping next to them tries to tuck them into a more convenient position. So a baby who is lively should definitely sleep in his own bed, both for his own and his parents' sakes. Don't worry about his moving around a lot. It's something that comes and goes, generally increasing when a baby has a lot going on during the day.

It's also true that babies who are active and in constant motion are often not very interested in a hug when they are wide awake so parents of such children may start to bring their half-asleep babies into their bed for some cuddles. For some parents, this may be the only time of day when they have physical contact for more than a few seconds at a time. The problem with this approach is that babies who have an impulsive streak are often unwilling to settle for only sometimes being allowed into their parents' bed. They have trouble learning that something is allowed but only within certain limits. They typically start to want to join their parents earlier and earlier in the morning with the result that they end up moving there completely. Many of these babies will accept a time limit only when they are a little older and more mature.

Keep in mind that the goal of sleep is rest. You need to set things up so that both you and your baby get as much rest as possible when you sleep.

Co-sleeping not an option

Your baby should definitely not sleep in the parental bed if one or both parents:	
✗	Have drunk alcohol or used any medicines or other substances with a narcotic effect.
✗	Are ill.
✗	Sleep on a mattress that you can sink deeply into, such as a waterbed.
✗	Smoke. Even if you never smoke in the bedroom, it appears that compounds in tobacco can linger on smokers' skin and hair and have a negative effect on a baby who comes into contact with them.

A room of his own

Many parents wonder when it is best to move their baby into his own room. When this move happens tends to vary somewhat from place to place.

Most experts agree that a newborn (up to four months) should spend the night in his parents' room as this is when cot death (see page 76) is most likely to occur. Studies have shown that a baby's heartbeat and breathing are more regular during the first weeks of life if he sleeps near his parents.

A good time for your baby to move into his own room is when he is between five and eight months old. At this age, your baby will be old enough to stop feeding at night, yet young enough so that he won't wonder where you are if you go out of his room. (This usually starts when a child is nearer nine months of age and although some babies don't appear to wonder about this, others will show by their behaviour that they do.)

If your baby is active and inventive, it is a good idea to put him in his own room before he learns how to stand up. If he sleeps in your room, he will become even more active as he will be able to see you when he stands up in his bed half asleep, and is less likely to settle himself down again to sleep.

I also recommend putting a baby who is easily distracted and wakes readily in a separate room early on.

Young babies don't usually complain about being in their own rooms but some eight- or nine-month-old babies do start to worry that their parents are gone forever if they are not in sight (this is often called separation anxiety; see page 117). An alternative solution,

Own room recommended

Your baby should sleep in his own room when:

He wakes up at the slightest noise.

He always wakes up when you come into your bedroom to sleep.

He has trouble seeing you without asking for something.

One of you wakes up at your baby's slightest movement and thus starts to attend to him before it's necessary.

if you want or have to keep your baby with you for longer, is to move your baby into his own room between 16 and 18 months. At this age, separation anxiety (if it has been distracting your baby) is easing. However, some children are affected for longer – up to two or three years of age and, for children like this who don't like sleeping on their own, I often recommend that they sleep in a room with a sibling if they have one, or even with a pet cat or a dog.

Moreover, any excitement about being able to stand and walk around has passed, and your baby will not be practising them as much as before so is usually sleeping more calmly. A baby is more active in his sleep when he practises a new skill like standing up or walking, which probably also affects his dreams although we don't know this for certain.

The box on the previous page sets out some additional reasons why it might be especially advisable to move a baby into his own room or into a room with his siblings.

PARENTAL DISAGREEMENTS

Although I've explained that it's important to make choices about certain sleeping arrangements, you and your partner may not always agree about these choices. This isn't surprising as we usually choose parenting methods and approaches that suit us as individuals, for example, those that we know from our own childhood. It is, however, very important for you and your partner to find a quiet moment – like a weekend morning – to sit down and discuss the issue(s), instead of debating how to deal with your baby when he wakes up in the middle of the night.

In discussing any situation, you need to try to put your baby's needs first, because he is an individual whose needs may be different from yours. This can be hard for some people. Putting yourself in another's shoes (whether a baby's or a partner's) isn't always easy. Very relaxed parents can have hot-headed babies who try from the very beginning to push their limits and very strict parents, who want to have fixed rules for everything, can give birth to babies who benefit more from a gentle and relaxed approach in their upbringing. It's easiest for everyone when children are similar to their parents and have similar needs. A family full of strong, but divergent, characters can pose a real challenge.

Single parents

In this book I often recommend that the father switches roles with the mother and takes care of the child for the first nights when teaching new and better sleeping habits. However, family circumstances vary, so what can a single parent or someone who cannot switch roles (if one partner is working away from home, or works night shifts, for example) do?

In general, when it comes to improving or changing a child's sleep, it helps if someone other than the primary carer (usually the mother) takes care of the child for the first few nights. While not absolutely necessary, it will make changing poor sleep habits easier.

SOME PRACTICAL HELP

A lone parent determined to change a child's sleeping habits can take advantage of all the advice in this book, as long as he or she ignores the guidance on switching roles. If you are in this position, you should be prepared for this change to be more difficult than if you were able to share the workload. The following are some points that could help you.

Do something for yourself

If you can, I would recommend that your child sleeps over at a relative's or trusted friend's house for one night before you start. Use this time to get some rest and do something that makes you feel good. Don't start doing housework!

Choose a sympathetic person to talk to

Look for support from friends, even if they cannot come and help you at home. Maybe they can give you support by discussing the situation. Don't bother talking to people you know will not support what you are doing.

Get assistance during the day

Although your friends or family may not be able to help you out at night, maybe they can help during the day. It is much easier for you to face the night work with your baby if you know that someone is going to take him in the morning and you are going to get some peace and quiet (and sleep).

Put other work aside

Before starting, do as much household and other work as you can and prepare to let things slide for a few days. For example, plan to have simple suppers rather than elaborate meals.

Change the environment

When trying to solve a baby's sleep problem, it usually helps a lot to also make some changes in his environment. Although you cannot change who puts your baby to bed and sees to him at night, you can make changes to other things. For example, you can move your baby's bed – either within the same room, to another room, or to another home (a helpful friend may lend you a room) for some nights.

Also, it helps to change what you and your baby do during the 15 or 20 minutes before he goes to sleep. By changing these things, you help your baby learn new things in new surroundings, which most people, including babies, find easier. You and your baby are in this together so both of you need to learn some new behaviour. For example, if your baby is used to being fed when he wakes up crying during the night because you go to him as fast as you can and give him a bottle so both of you can hopefully get some sleep again, this behaviour needs to change. You cannot change your baby's behaviour (because you cannot reason with him) but you can change your own behaviour. You can also make it easier for your baby by adjusting the timings of his sleep (see also chapter 4).

Be a little distant

If your child sleeps in your room, you should sleep in the living room (or another room), at least until he wakes up. Sleeping in the same room as your child means your presence can easily wake him (even if you are quiet, it is not noise but your presence that is disturbing).

If your baby is still breastfeeding, try not to hold him the same way you do when breastfeeding as you put him to bed or when you take him in your arms at night. Hold him facing away from you, or against your shoulder, when you are not actually breastfeeding.

Have a nice day

Make the days during which you are working on a sleep problem as fun as possible. Make your time together as good as it gets. Babies are nearly always happier in the open air than inside, so spend as much time outdoors as possible. Here I am not talking about going shopping! I am talking about going outside with your child to play or discover the world in a manner suitable to your baby's age, temperament and abilities.

Communicating with a baby

The spoken word is a poor tool for communicating with your baby; it's your overall behaviour that grabs his attention. Small babies have a very limited understanding of spoken language. Around one year of age, your baby will probably understand single words but not sentences, and soon he will start to understand two words together. As he grows older, he will, of course, learn even more words. However, even when a baby can grasp and understand single words, he still works out the meaning of what is said mostly from how it is said. Babies pay attention to tone and vocal nuances and get more from that than from the words themselves.

Babies learn most of all from body language. Body language is a big part of the way babies understand others and express themselves. They use eye contact very purposefully. Not very long after birth, it's already possible to communicate with your baby by looking into his eyes. Right from the beginning, therefore, it's good to get your baby used to you looking in his eyes when you speak to him. This will help him to focus, strengthens his self-image, and teaches him to listen. It's often fun to see how children use eye contact. For example, if an adult tells a one-year-old child not to do something, he may look away from the adult or even just close his eyes. In effect, he is saying 'I'm not listening to you, and if I can't see you, then I can't hear you either.'

It's good to be a little dramatic or theatrical when communicating with your baby. You need to keep in mind how he understands what you do and say.

Babies are sensitive to others' feelings, and very young babies especially so. They can work out your state of mind. Most parents know from experience that, for example, if they are trying to get a baby to fall asleep quickly, and try hard not to let him notice this, it's almost certain that the baby will sense that something is different and will instead take even longer than usual to get to sleep. This sensitivity to feelings has a big impact on baby-parent communication, and it's one of the main reasons you need to pay attention to your own welfare. If you are very tired or feeling poorly for any reason, this will affect your baby and his wellbeing.

How to 'speak' to your baby

Gestures rather than words are important to young babies (under a year). Therefore:

If you want to say	You should
I love you so much.	Look gently into his eyes and stroke his head.
Wow, I'm amazed you can do that!	Gasp in amazement, act out how surprised you are, and stretch your arms out, palms up, to show it.
I'm your friend!	Tip your head to one side and stretch one arm out, palm up. If your baby is scared or shy, approach him from the side and don't look too directly into his eyes, so he doesn't feel threatened. Instead, glance at him with upturned palms.

How babies sleep

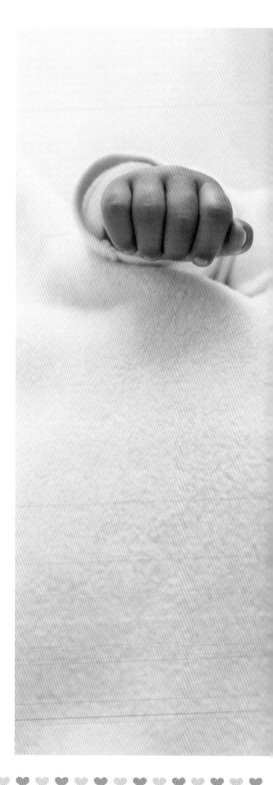

There is still a lot we don't know about sleep; its exact purpose and the role of its various stages, for example, are still not completely clear. But both our understanding of sleep, and the human need for it, have moved forward over the years, and it's good to keep in mind some of what has been learned when you care for your baby.

The different stages of sleep

For both adults and babies, there are two kinds of sleep: REM and non-REM sleep.

REM SLEEP

This type of sleep is distinguished by 'rapid eye movements', hence its name. During this stage of sleep, a person's eyes quiver under closed lids. REM is the stage of sleep when we dream and electroencephalograms (EEGs) show that during REM sleep, our brains are about as active as when we are awake, even though our bodies are resting. Although an occasional twitch or movement can be observed during REM sleep, for the most part it's as if the body is paralysed. And there's good reason for this; if we weren't immobilised, because of what we are dreaming, we might move around so much that we could hurt ourselves.

Researchers believe that during REM sleep we work through and process the lessons and experiences of the previous day. It is, therefore, not surprising that babies, who are experiencing and working through many, many things for the first time, spend more time in REM sleep than adults. A newborn baby spends about 50 per cent of the night in REM sleep, and premature babies even more. Adults, by contrast, spend about 20 per cent of the night in REM sleep.

NON-REM SLEEP

There are four stages of non-REM sleep, characterised by the depth of sleep – the first level is very light and the fourth is very deep. As you sleep more and more deeply, your brain activity lessens until it becomes very slow and tranquil. Your body also relaxes – as body movements are often correlated with your state of mind – but in this stage of sleep, your body is not semi-paralysed, as in REM sleep.

During deep non-REM sleep, babies can move around more than during REM sleep. The most active ones can move quite a lot, but their movements are usually slow and generally purposeless.

SLEEP CYCLES

When your baby sleeps, she moves through the various stages of sleep, just as adults do. From the time she falls asleep in the evening until she wakes up in the morning, she is constantly passing from stage to stage. This means, for example, progressing from light sleep to deep sleep and then back to light sleep again, a process called a sleep cycle.

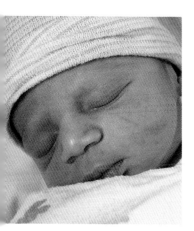

Typical sleep cycles

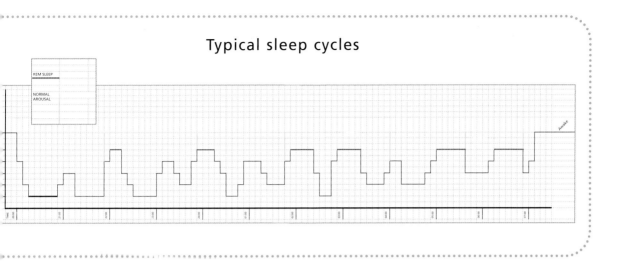

These cycles are not always identical. Earlier in the night adults spend longer in deep sleep (non-REM stage 4), while later in the night we spend more time in REM sleep.

The length of each sleep cycle increases as babies grow older. During the first year of life, each cycle lasts about 40–60 minutes. By the age of three, this length has increased to about 90 minutes and stays at that level up to adulthood.

It's well known that babies in the first months of life move very quickly through stages 1 and 2 and so reach very deep sleep quite fast. This means that they won't wake up if, for example, they are laid down or moved from one place to another.

With most babies, the length of the stages changes as they grow, and slowly it starts to take babies 10–20 minutes to reach deep sleep. Parents then typically start to say that their baby has become more sensitive, and that it's harder to lay her down after she falls asleep on the breast or in a parent's arms.

It's good to keep this change in mind from the beginning, and to get your baby used to not always being able to fall asleep in your arms, but rather to be put in her cot while awake and to fall asleep there without assistance.

NIGHT WAKING

In the lighter stages of sleep (REM sleep and non-REM stages 1 and 2), your baby will slip out of sleep every now and then. This may happen in every sleep cycle throughout the whole night, and it is a natural aspect of sleep. Your baby wakes slightly, moves about and perhaps opens her eyes, looks around and then, ideally, closes her eyes and goes back to sleep. Usually you aren't aware of this and imagine that your baby is fast asleep, which is good for all concerned. This is

This printout of a night's sleep for a newborn shows that the baby's sleep is cyclical. Initially she falls into a deep sleep then throughout the night, she moves through the different stages of non-REM sleep into REM sleep, when she dreams (indicated in red). The yellow 'spikes' are periods when she is more aroused and comes closer to a waking state than a sleeping one.

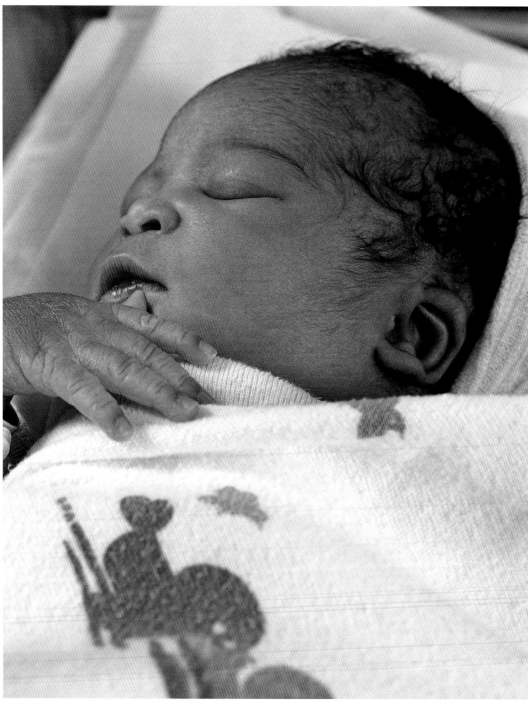

particularly true when she wakes early in the night. As your baby hasn't been asleep for long and is less likely to fully rouse herself, you will tend not to notice these brief awakenings. But with some babies, these awakenings can be noisy affairs: your baby may cry, laugh, talk, roll over on to all sides, and practise everything she knows how to do, and yet still be more asleep than awake. It's therefore very important not to interfere with this natural aspect of sleep too quickly. Instead, you should first give your baby time to fall back asleep by herself.

But not all babies can go back to sleep after waking during the night. Instead of turning over and falling asleep again, some babies become more alert, wake up fully, and cry out for their parents' help to get back to sleep. This is one of the most frequent sleep difficulties that babies experience. Most commonly, a baby can fall back asleep early in the night, but later on, she will find it harder and harder to do so. This situation is made more difficult to correct by the fact that towards morning, babies spend more time in light-sleep phases. Thus you should wait longer to help your baby early in the night, when it's more likely that she will get back to sleep on her own, but it makes more sense to spring into action more quickly later in the night, as

Night-time waking

The following factors increase the likelihood that your baby will rouse herself fully when she wakes up at night:	
✗	She cannot fall asleep on her own in the evening.
✗	She falls asleep somewhere other than where she is when she wakes up (for example, she falls asleep in the living room and wakes up in her bed).
✗	She doesn't feel well (due to illness or some other reason).
✗	She has reached some new developmental stage (particularly in her motor development) and may start to practise her skills during the lighter stages of sleep.
✗	A parent is not feeling well (and the baby senses this).
✗	One of her parents is a very light sleeper and goes to her very quickly when she makes any noise.

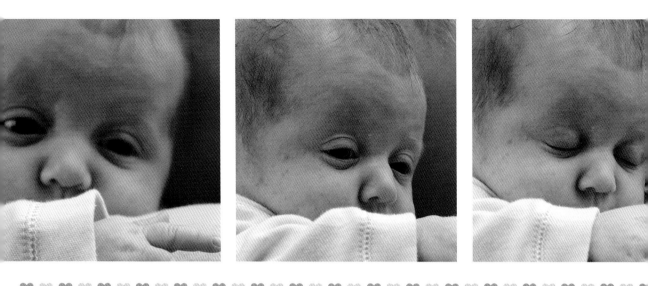

otherwise your baby is more likely to rouse herself fully and want to start the day.

Babies who need their parents' help to fall asleep in the evening are more likely to wake up fully when they slip out of sleep during the night. It actually doesn't matter what kind of help the parents provide – often, a baby will fall asleep while drinking from a bottle in her bed (which counts as help, even though it's indirect) or while breastfeeding in her mother's arms – but much more limited assistance can also have an effect. A parent sitting with the baby, stroking her hair and humming a song, until the baby is completely asleep, may work just as well. The older a baby gets, the more likely it becomes that she will want the same evening 'help' repeated when she half-wakes up at night, although this varies from baby to baby. Some babies who get help falling asleep in the evening never call for a parent at night, but the chances that calling will happen do increase as a baby grows and matures.

It's good to keep all of this in mind when reading the age-specific chapter 4 (see pages 70–131). In particular, it helps to know that if your baby rouses herself slightly at night, this is normal and usually will not lead to her waking up fully.

"You should wait longer to help your baby early in the night ... but it makes sense to respond more quickly later in the night..."

Development and sleep

A baby's growth and development often account for her reactions and how she receives and processes messages and stimuli, but babies vary as to when they reach each level of maturity. Babies can mature quickly in one area and slowly in another; for example, speedy motor development isn't always paired with swift cognitive development, and vice versa.

MOTOR DEVELOPMENT

Any leap forward in your baby's motor skills – learning to roll over, stand or walk, for example – may disturb her sleep. Once a skill is mastered, your baby may start to wake up at night and/or become less willing to go to sleep in the evening. Cheerful, enthusiastic babies who have just learned to stand up on their own may practise their new skills whenever they have the chance – even during light-sleep stages in the middle of the night. Ideally, you should react to this behaviour by emphasising your child's ability to solve her problems independently, for example, by learning to lie down on her own if she stands up repeatedly.

Your baby's stage of development is also vital in assessing sleep-related accident risks. You want to be certain that if you leave your sleeping baby alone for any length of time, she won't roll out of the parental bed or climb out of her cot.

COGNITIVE DEVELOPMENT

Slowly but surely, your baby will come to realise that her actions affect the world around her. She will sense that her behaviour influences the behaviour of others, and starts to explore how this works. She will discover that when she does something, such as crying or coughing, something else happens, too, like Mummy or Daddy coming. This new ability to see how one thing follows another can be used to influence your baby's sleeping habits. She can learn, for example, that "Whenever Daddy sits in this chair with me and sings this song, I get put to bed afterwards." When your baby cries while being put to bed, you probably worry that she doesn't want to be left alone. In fact, she is most likely not afraid of being left on her own, but just wants to stay awake rather than go to sleep; she's complaining about being put to bed because of her enthusiasm for life awake.

Some babies start to show a fear of strangers between four and eight months of age. (This is often confused with separation anxiety, which is a different phenomenon, see pages 34 and 117). At this stage,

your baby's horizons are expanding and she is forming clearer opinions about what kind of people and conduct she does and doesn't like. For example, babies are often afraid of people with a particular appearance, such as bearded men. If picked up by anyone other than their parents, babies frequently express their fears vociferously by crying loudly. This issue is unlikely to disturb your baby's actual sleep, but it could mean that she will start to have an opinion about whether it's Mummy or Daddy who should lay her down to sleep or bring her a dummy at night. If your baby starts to discriminate between you and your partner, it's best not to comply with her wishes because there is a risk that she will try the same control tactics during the day, maybe over who feeds or dresses her.

Separation anxiety

As they get older, some babies can start to feel anxious or afraid when they are left alone. The reason is that a baby does not yet understand that things that disappear from sight continue to exist. If Daddy goes out of sight, say, your baby may be unsure whether he still exists or whether he is gone for good. The term for this is separation anxiety and it will generally pass within a few months. Babies differ quite a lot in when and whether they show separation anxiety; it appears most often between the ages of nine and 15 months. Some experts consider separation anxiety the main cause of sleep problems in babies, but this is making too much of the issue. Sometimes, a baby is just trying to exert control over her environment.

If your goal is to get your baby used to sleeping alone in the bedroom, or to move her to her own room, you need to take separation anxiety into account. Bear in mind that separation anxiety is evoked not just by a baby's mother or father, but by everyone to whom a baby is attached. However, the problem may lie elsewhere; your baby might object to sleeping on her own simply because she doesn't want to be left alone.

There is an easy way to test whether your baby is experiencing separation anxiety but it's best if someone other than her mother carries it out, as a baby might cry for her mum without being affected by separation anxiety. It's also good to do this early in the day when your baby is feeling alert.

Start while your baby is playing in a room. The person looking after her leaves the room, and makes sure that your baby knows this (waves bye-bye or says "Good-bye"). A baby with separation anxiety will immediately start to complain loudly or to follow, making sure that her carer remains in sight.

If your baby shows separation anxiety, you may need to adjust your behaviour accordingly. With a baby who, all of a sudden, starts to

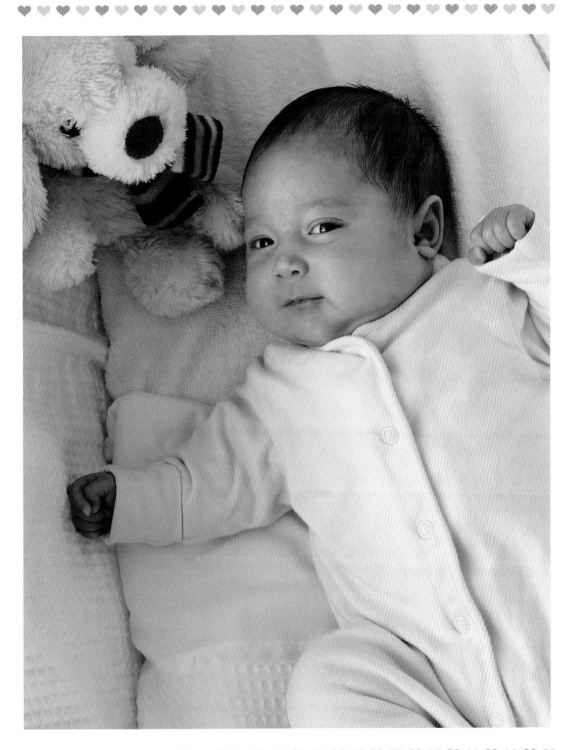

complain vehemently if she is put to bed alone, even if she has fallen asleep alone for months, it's best to sit near her, perhaps in the doorway, while she is falling asleep. But avoid staying too close to her, because you may be tempted to do more than just sitting with her. We all have a strong tendency to want to speed up a baby's falling asleep and, in order to do this, you might be tempted to touch your baby or respond to her in other ways. But these gestures will disturb the process even more. If your baby has separation anxiety, stick to just being in the same room with her – it's your calm presence she needs.

Developing a sense of self

After nine months in the womb, a baby needs time to realise that she is an independent being. To start with, she regards herself and her mother as a single being. Slowly she learns that she is one individual and her mother another. A baby usually works this out during the first months of life, without being aware of the process. It's best for this discovery to take place automatically, through her seeing and experiencing that people besides Mummy care for her now and then. Sometimes, Mummy goes out of the room for a moment and everything is still OK.

Some babies have trouble going through this process of separation, and the later it takes place, the harder it appears to be for the baby. This is particularly noticeable with babies who are frequently alone with their mothers. A baby's separation from her mother is considered a prerequisite for her developing a sense of self and her own independence. Babies with separation problems don't want to take their eyes off their mothers and such a situation can become very burdensome for mother and baby, and affect a baby's wellbeing. The main feature of such an interaction is the baby's desire for her life to be completely interwoven with her mother's, and the relationship starts to become very stressful. The baby's sleep may be disturbed as she wakes up repeatedly to check whether Mummy is nearby.

When evaluating sleep problems, you need to take separation from the mother into account – both in planning who cares for your baby and how such care takes place. It may be necessary to involve more people in your baby's daily care, and her father will be important in this process. If he is not around much (or at all), you will need to call on someone else who you trust to help out. Now and then, for example, you could ask the baby's grandfather to change her nappy and hold her, or her aunt to feed her and play with her, or have a babysitter look after her regularly, say for a couple of hours.

If your baby doesn't take well to this, begin slowly, ideally with an alternative carer just playing with her the first few times. Doing this in your home means that you can stay in sight – at least initially. The next step is for the other carer to change your baby, then feed her, and finally to put her to bed. This approach gives your baby time to get used to people other than her mother taking care of her.

Separating a baby from her mother is not only a project for your baby but also, and no less so, for you. For various reasons, you may find it difficult to relax your grip or to give your baby the necessary time and space to develop an independent sense of self. If the separation process is not easy, you may start to feel insecure if your baby cries and begin to lack trust in your parenting instincts. If this is the case, support from someone who understands – a friend, relative or professional – will be invaluable and can help you through difficult times.

Fear of the dark

Parents often worry that their baby is afraid of the dark, particularly if they were once afraid of the dark themselves and remember how difficult it was. Some parents start to think about this when their baby is only three or four months old, but little babies are not cognitively mature enough to be afraid of the dark.

Year-old babies may just have started to show they might be afraid of the dark but a baby of this age could actually be feeling separation anxiety (see pages 34 and 117), which is completely different: a baby with separation anxiety is afraid to be left alone regardless of whether it is light or dark.

Babies who are just a few months old can start to cry when the light is turned off, but this is because they connect darkness with having to go to sleep. If they are not happy about having to go to sleep, they may start to cry. This varies from baby to baby though. If you find that your baby is calmer if it's not completely dark when she goes to sleep, by all means leave a little light on. Always keep in mind, however, that when your baby wakes during the night, she wants to see the same things that were around her when she fell asleep. If she sleeps all night without waking up, you need not worry about this but if she tends to wake up during the night, it is advisable not to turn off any lights that were on when she fell asleep. Leave them on all night but keep the room as dim as possible.

"Real fear of the dark requires a certain level of maturity and experience, and does not usually happen until after the age of two, if at all."

How feeding affects sleep

Food and sleep tend to be considerably intertwined in babies' lives. Meal timings and routines often affect sleep; babies who fall asleep while feeding in the evening, for example, are more likely to wake up during the night. Moreover, many studies have shown that breastfed babies are more likely to wake up more often at night and until an older age than babies who are bottlefed. This finding has, understandably, not been popular, as it threatens to make breastfeeding less attractive. After all, breast milk is the food that nature designed for babies and that they ought to receive, if possible, for the first six months of their life. But you can train a breastfed baby to sleep at night just as you can train a bottlefed baby.

Many parents complain about getting inconsistent advice, including advice about breastfeeding and sleeping habits, but you need to assess what works best for you and your baby in order to choose the most effective approach.

BREASTFEEDING

A breastfed baby has no more need for night-time feeds than a bottlefed baby. The reason that breastfed babies wake up more often at night probably has nothing to do with nutrition, but rather with the routines and habits involved in breastfeeding. It is quite likely that it's mothers' own insecurity that is responsible for the higher rate of night-time feeding among breastfed babies.

Research has shown that night-time feeding is the strongest factor in a baby's continuing to wake up frequently at night. This connection between night-time feeding and night-time waking becomes more and more noticeable as a baby gets older. Around four months of age, babies often start waking up more frequently and feeding more at night. At six or seven months of age, this tendency becomes even more noticeable. Those babies who wake up to feed start to explore how far they can push things or, as they might say, "How often will they allow me to feed?" or "Well, if I can feed once, could I maybe feed three times? Why not try?"

With most babies older than six or seven months, night-time feeding is probably just a habit. Babies get stuck in a pattern where, if they wake, they get help falling back to sleep. Often this assistance consists of being fed, because for most parents, that is the quickest way to get their babies to fall asleep again (though it is also the way that most promotes continued night-time waking). Feeding a baby who has woken up is an understandable reaction on the part of tired

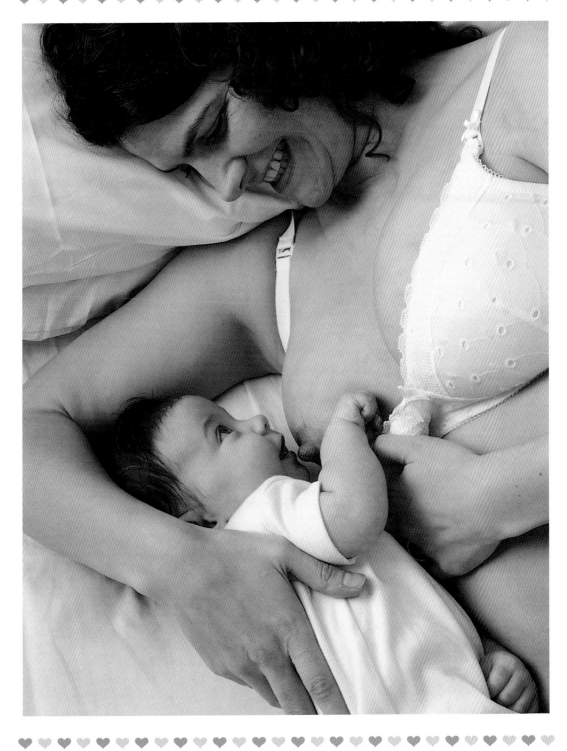

"There's often a strong link between babies' sleeping rhythms and feeding schedules."

parents, yet it is important to understand that a baby who falls asleep in the evening while feeding will be more likely to ask to feed during the night. It is common for babies to want at night what they had while falling asleep in the evening. That said, some babies fall asleep while feeding and sleep well all night and with these babies, it's not necessary to put a full stop to letting them fall asleep while feeding. But it's good to bear in mind that a baby who falls asleep while sucking on her bottle is more likely to ask for it during the night if some factor, such as illness, disturbs her regular sleeping patterns. In short, falling asleep while feeding is a risk factor, but one that doesn't necessarily lead to problems, especially not with babies who are healthy, calm and tractable by nature. Also consider the health of your baby's developing teeth; experts suggest it is not good for a baby to fall asleep with her teeth bathed in milk.

Sleeping rhythms and feeding schedules are linked. Babies who want to feed frequently and in small amounts tend to want to sleep frequently and in small amounts, while babies whose sleeping habits are irregular tend to eat and drink at irregular times, too. Bringing more order to a baby's feeding schedule will often have a positive effect on her sleeping rhythms.

SOLID FOOD BEFORE SLEEP

A baby should neither go to bed hungry nor with too full a tummy. If your baby has started eating solid food once a day, she should have this meal an hour or two before going to sleep at night. When you add a second meal, this should be in the middle of the day. The third meal should then be added in the afternoon. When your baby moves up to eating solid food four times a day, meals should be served in the morning, at midday and around dinner time with a little snack before going to sleep.

Dinner should, ideally, be a relatively large meal and served on the early side, say around 6 p.m., with a bedtime snack an hour or two later. Big meals perk babies up, so it's a good idea to ensure that the energy from dinner finds an outlet in play before your baby is settled for sleep. As for the snack, your baby needs something light and warm in her tummy before going to sleep. She'll then sleep better and you will feel more confident about saying "No" to food or milk during the night.

An evening snack should include natural carbohydrates, for example, grains, dairy products or fruit. For a little baby, warm porridge is a good option (when she is old enough, at around six months). One-year-old babies can have unsweetened breakfast cereal with milk, a slice of bread and a glass of milk, or plain yogurt with fruit or unsweetened fruit yogurt.

Don't give a baby heavy or sweet foods such as sweetened grain products, flavoured milk, sweet biscuits or cake. Make snack time an opportunity to keep your child company at the table; have something yourself and use the time to have a chat.

Between the age of six and 12 months, it's important for your baby to progressively and, in the end, completely disconnect sleep and food. The goal is for her to stop falling asleep while feeding. By working on this from the very beginning, and taking care that your baby falls asleep more and more often without feeding, it's possible to stop her from getting stuck in the mistaken idea that the only way to fall asleep is to feed.

Bedtime porridge

While you can use a prepared porridge mix, which does not need to be boiled but simply mixed with water or milk, you can make your own. Porridge can be made from various types of grain and flour.

To 100 g of oatmeal, add 300 ml of water (you can make more or less, but always follow these proportions). Boil together and stir constantly for 3 minutes.

For small babies it's good to stir with a whisk, which makes the oatmeal softer.

If you like, you can sweeten the oatmeal with fruit purée but don't add sugar or salt.

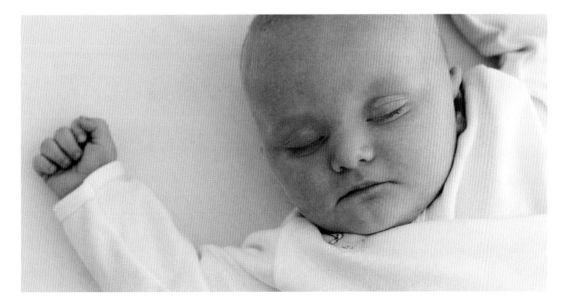

Realistic expectations

One of the biggest developmental processes babies undergo involves forming a regular daily rhythm of wakefulness and sleep – this is technically called a circadian rhythm. Daily rhythms appear to develop in varying ways for each individual. Some babies seem to almost automatically pick up the habit of sleeping more at night and staying awake longer during the day. Others make their parents struggle to teach them the difference between night and day.

Parents tend to judge when their baby has started to sleep through the night based on when their baby stops waking them up. But one study, which used video recordings to observe babies all night long, showed that at around a year of age, the vast majority of babies woke up, at least partially, for brief periods (see page 29). However, not all these babies woke up their parents or needed their parents' help to fall asleep again. Grasping this is very important, as a baby's ability to go back to sleep after having woken up at night usually depends on the ability to fall asleep on her own in the evening. The issue is basically whether a baby has the capacity to fall asleep without help.

A small baby (less than a year old) who has started to sleep through the night can sometimes become mixed up and lose her proper rhythm. She will start to wake up more frequently at night, and can have trouble getting back into a routine again.

HOW LONG DO BABIES SLEEP?

You need to know what you can expect from your baby in terms of sleep. The table on the opposite page shows the average time in hours and minutes that babies sleep at various ages, both at night and during the day. This data comes from my own research, and is consistent with the results from other studies of sleep length and the distribution of sleep time between night and day.

Bear in mind that these are averages for a large group of babies. In the oldest group, for example, some of the children had completely stopped sleeping during the day, which explains why the average length of daytime sleep at this age was only six minutes a day. The average amount of sleep in a 24-hour period decreases as children grow older but this decrease takes place entirely during the daytime. The length of night-time sleep appears to stay constant from six months of age until babies stop taking a daytime nap, at which point it increases slightly.

How long does an average baby sleep?

Age	Night-time sleep	Daytime sleep	Total sleep	Normal sleep range
6–8 months	10 hrs 54 mins	3 hrs 42 mins	14 hrs 36 mins	13½–16 hrs
9–14 months	10 hrs 48 mins	2 hrs 54 mins	13 hrs 42 mins	12½–15½ hrs
15–23 months	11 hrs	1 hr 48 mins	12 hrs 48 mins	11½–15½ hrs
24–48 months	11 hrs 30 mins	6 mins	11 hrs 36 mins	10½–13 hrs

Sleep timings

Parents often worry that their baby doesn't get enough sleep. But there's usually more reason to look at when a baby sleeps rather than how much. The timing of sleep influences how well a baby sleeps. A baby who takes a nap at the 'wrong' time and wakes up during the night, can start to sleep much better at night just by fixing or changing the timings of her naps. What, though, is a 'wrong' time for a nap? The most common cases of 'wrong' nap times involve a baby staying awake for either too long or too short a time before going to bed for the night. Parents of school-age children know very well that they shouldn't let a child fall asleep late in the day as she will then sleep poorly during the night. This also applies to babies. A baby should not be allowed to nap too close to the end of the day although, of course, the end of the day comes earlier for her than for an older child. It's also clear that babies who take two or more daytime naps should start their first nap neither too early nor too late. In short, the periods of wakefulness before a baby takes her first daytime nap and before she goes to sleep in the evening are very important. Nonetheless, if your baby naps at different times from those suggested in this book, and still sleeps well at night, then you should definitely not change your baby's sleep rhythms.

Periods of wakefulness

The table on page 44 suggests sensible lengths of time in hours and minutes for these two periods of wakefulness at different ages. (Chapter 4 on pages 70–131 offers more detail on this issue.)

You should also look at the number of naps your baby takes; a baby aged four to six months is going from three naps down to two. At 10 to 15 months, the number of naps goes from two down to one. When children stop sleeping during the day varies tremendously. Indeed, it can be at any age from 18 months to five years. But continuing to have a period of quiet time in the middle of the day is a good idea, even for children who have stopped napping. Quiet time can mean snuggling under a blanket and listening to music or reading a story.

Recommended length of time spent awake

Age	Number of hours awake before the first daytime nap	Number of hours awake before going to bed at night
4 months	1 hr 30 mins – 2 hrs	about 2½
6 months	2 hrs – 2 hrs 30 mins	about 3½
9 months	2 hrs 30 mins – 3 hrs	about 4
15 months	3–4 hrs	5–7
24 months	4 hrs	6–8

Babies who have been ill for an extended time or who are physically or mentally challenged have different benchmarks from other children of a similar age. This applies both to waking and sleeping times and to the number of naps they take. A 15-month-old baby who has had frequent long stays in hospital, for example, might behave more like a six-month-old baby in terms of sleeping and waking times. You have to take into consideration illnesses or disabilities that affect a baby's endurance. But these babies have just as much need as other children for a certain amount of rhythm and regularity in their sleeping patterns so that they can sleep as well as possible.

LEARNING TO FALL ASLEEP ALONE

How realistic is it to expect a baby of any given age to learn to fall asleep on her own in her own bed, as opposed to having a parent present? By having a parent present, I mean that the baby can see a parent or parent-like figure while she falls asleep. The answer appears to be somewhat age dependent. Some babies aged nine to 14 months do need a parent's presence to be able to fall asleep. This need is tied to separation anxiety and is something they grow out of.

When your baby needs you to be there, be sure not to do more for her than just being there; for example, don't pat her or sing to her so that she falls asleep more quickly. Slowly but surely, reduce the amount of time you stay with her. Normally, when your baby can handle your disappearing from sight during the day, you can also start to leave her field of vision in the evening before she actually falls asleep. It's usually easiest for all if this is something that's introduced slowly. First try to leave your baby alone for a moment during the day, and when she tolerates this well, try to leave her in the evening, after putting her to bed.

44 HOW BABIES SLEEP

Leaving your baby alone

There are two possible ways of encouraging your baby to fall asleep on her own. The idea behind the first method is to teach your baby to trust that you will come back – and come back not because she is crying for you, but because you said you would.

Method two involves fading away gradually until only your voice remains until it, too, stops. Your voice is a powerful and calming tool to use when settling your baby down to sleep for the night.

An evening routine

Settling your baby to sleep on her own should be part of a recognisable evening routine. This may involve a calming bath, a final snack or feed and a story, then a move into the bedroom. All these cues tell your baby that it is time for sleep. Close the curtains, have a final cuddle, then put your baby in her cot and turn off the light. Say "Night night" and then try one of these approaches.

Method 1

If your baby is well over a year old you need to give her some reason why you are leaving, but keep it simple so that she understands. For example, say that you're getting a chair or going to the bathroom.

Leave the room so that your baby cannot see you for 10 seconds. It's good if she can tell where you are – say or do something that she can hear. Then come back in and sit quietly on a chair, without talking, until your baby falls asleep.

In short, leave the room once, soon after putting your baby to bed, and stay outside briefly. Then slowly lengthen the time you stay outside your baby's room. After several evenings of this, hopefully your baby will stop waiting for you, turn away and continue to settle down towards sleep.

Method 2

Keep the door to baby's room open, as in the previous method but in this approach, locate yourself just outside the doorway in a place where your baby still can see you. You might be folding clean clothes or doing something else which requires you to move around, but you never go far away. It's good if your baby can always hear you, so you might sing or hum a song.

Then you locate yourself nearly out of sight (maybe your baby can see your foot, for example), but still hear your voice. After a few nights, you sit out of sight but still let your baby hear your voice (you can talk on the phone or hum a song, for example). Then, after some nights, lower your voice or stop every now and then until you finally stop altogether.

"Your baby can learn to fall asleep without you being in sight, as long as she still can hear your voice."

POWER NAPS

Some babies grab bits of sleep – often no more than several minutes – here and there during the day, perhaps in the car or while they are supposed to be feeding. There is, however, a big risk that these 'power naps' will disturb their sleep at other times. Parents typically underestimate the effect of these brief snoozes: they are so short that a baby doesn't get a real rest out of them, but long enough that she recharges for two or three hours of wakefulness. As a baby gets older, these naps can disturb her sleep and wellbeing more and more, which may show up as crankiness or irritability.

There are various ways of preventing power naps. One is to avoid scheduling car rides between one and two hours after your baby wakes up, as babies often get drowsy around then. A routine that works for car trips is to take short trips just after your baby wakes up, but longer trips (of an hour or more) during your baby's normal nap time, so that she can nap in the car.

Babies under three or four months old are the ones who tend to doze while feeding. It's good when feeding your small baby to check that she is sucking. If you think she is nodding off, hold her against your shoulder, as when winding her, for a moment to wake her.

DUMMIES

Dummies are excellent tools for comforting a baby and are invaluable in caring for a baby who is ill or who cries a lot for some reason. Many parents ask for guidance on their use. Some worry that if a very young baby gets a dummy, it might promote a bad sucking style

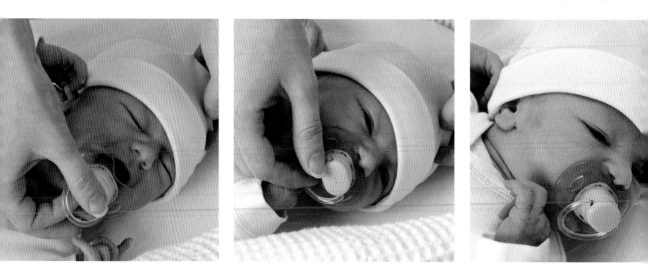

and lead to breastfeeding problems. Usually, these worries are unfounded. There are many, many examples of babies whose technique for latching on to the breast actually improves after they start to use a dummy. However, it's best not to offer a newborn a dummy for her first experience of sucking, but rather to offer the breast first and only then a dummy.

Always use a dummy in moderation as its use can prevent a baby expressing herself. Crying is a precursor to speaking, so if you always pop a dummy in your baby's mouth when she complains, you are telling her that she should stop communicating. Moreover, a baby's new teeth should not be in constant contact with a dummy.

You need to set definite rules for dummy use. For example, when your baby is eight months old, you can allow her a dummy when she sits in her car seat and also when she goes to sleep, but otherwise only in exceptional circumstances, like if she hurts herself. In this way your baby will get used to the idea that after waking up in the morning, she leaves her dummy in bed or brings it into the kitchen where it is kept on a particular shelf. Later, when she goes to sleep in the evening, you and she can get the dummy from the spot where it is kept. It is easy to teach your child routines like this.

Some parents find dummies useful when introducing their baby to solid food. To help a baby learn to swallow food, they may offer the dummy after giving a mouthful of food.

BEING OUTDOORS

All babies need to spend time outdoors – to see the world and to exercise their bodies. A good rule of thumb is that babies less than a year old should go outside once a day, while those more than a year old should go out twice a day. Take your one- to two year old outside once before her nap and once afterwards.

Dress your baby for the weather. It's not enough to just push the buggy or pram; take your baby in your arms and show her what's around you. When she is able, let her move around. The goal of time outdoors isn't to get her to fall asleep while you push the buggy down the street, but rather to let her get some fresh air and exercise.

"Time outdoors affects sleep. Babies and children, just like adults, sleep better after spending time in the fresh air."

Sleep problems

Trouble falling asleep and other sleep-related matters are very common; studies suggest that about 20 per cent of children under five years of age have a sleep problem. Some studies show, as well, that yet more children struggle with minor difficulties related to sleep and sleeping habits.

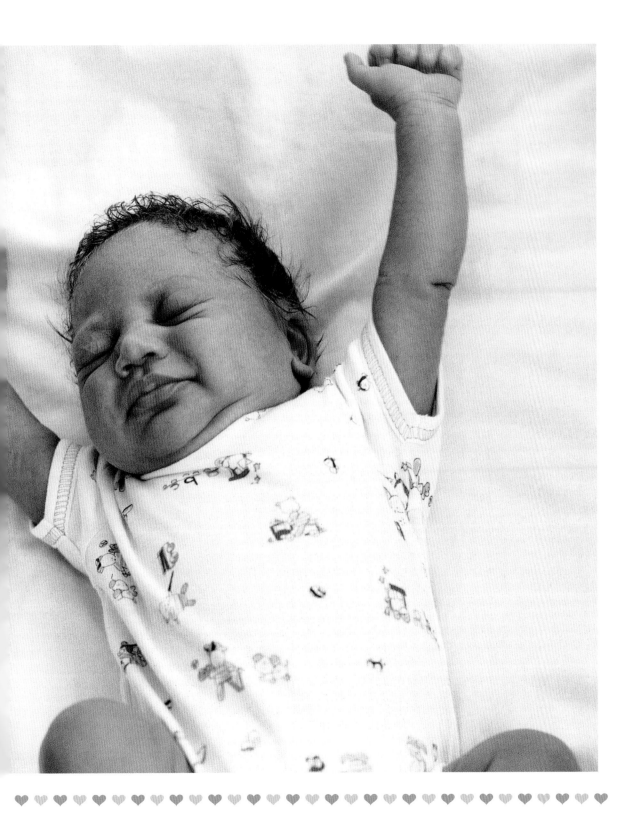

Why babies can't sleep

Why do some babies have sleep problems and others not? According to a study which I worked on with Marga Thome (formerly Dean and currently Professor at the Faculty of Nursing at the University of Iceland), the potential causes and factors can be divided into the five categories described on these pages. The factors are often intertwined – sleep problems can arise in a baby who is sensitive to distractions and who also has repeated ear infections, for example. Sometimes it is not possible to discern any one clear cause, and indeed there is still a lot we don't know about the causes of babies' sleep problems.

PHYSICAL ILLNESS OR PAIN

Sleeping patterns may be disrupted during an illness and may not return to normal even after a baby recovers. This can happen with any type of illness but most commonly with ear infections, allergies, reflux, asthma and chronic infections (see the discussion of illness and sleep in chapter 5, pages 132–41).

TEMPERAMENT

Newborns, who are very sensitive to distractions, are at a greater risk of sleep problems as are babies who are physically very active and those who don't have good daily rhythms; the latter are unable to recognise their own needs, such as that for sleep. They don't know they are sleepy or don't show it clearly (and when parents themselves are tired, the sleep needs of their child may be difficult to discern). Parents, too, can disrupt a baby's daily rhythms. If parents are not organised (don't adhere to specific feeding or sleeping times), they may interfere with their child's periods of sleepiness and wakefulness.

DEVELOPMENTAL FACTORS

Some factors that influence sleep are a result of immaturity while others result from mastering new skills. Problems can arise when a baby is unable to fall asleep on his own and needs help – being fed or rocked – to do so. Learning to soothe himself to sleep can take a baby some time (see also pages 73 and 95).

Sleep also may not seem so attractive to a baby when he learns new motor skills, like rolling over on to his tummy or standing up on his own (see also chapter 4, page 103). Similarly, sleep may be disturbed due to cognitive issues, which can distract or preoccupy babies. For example, four-month-old babies like to explore how they can produce various reactions from adults and may start asking for more assistance falling asleep or after night waking to elicit them. Babies around the age of one year can have trouble with separation anxiety, and then start getting anxious when they are 'asked' to fall asleep alone (see page 117).

ENVIRONMENTAL FACTORS

Both existing and impending factors in a family's daily life can disturb a baby's sleep. Examples include frequent moves or cramped housing, neighbours who complain about every little sound from the baby or the birth of a sibling.

PARENTAL FACTORS

Sleep problems are likely to be an issue where parents have little experience of taking care of babies and/or receive little outside support. There is a connection between babies' sleep problems and parental depression although researchers argue whether parental depression causes sleep problems or vice versa. Probably it varies from family to family. What we do know, however, is that in dealing with a child's sleep problem, it is also important to work on the parents' wellbeing at the same time. By doing so, it is more likely that a solution will be found for the problem, and that future sleep problems will be less likely.

Recognising there's a problem

There are five main signs of a sleep problem in babies and toddlers from birth to the age of two:

1 **Night-time wakefulness:** A baby wakes his parents up at night more often than is normal for his age.

2 **Difficulty falling asleep:** A baby needs a long time to fall asleep, or needs more assistance than his age and level of development would suggest.

3 **Difficulties with daytime naps:** A baby naps irregularly or for short periods (less than 45 minutes at a time).

4 **Out-of-sync sleep timings:** A baby's 'night' begins and ends at a non-standard time, for example runs from 5 a.m. to noon.

5 **Daytime irritability:** A baby is cranky and tired and has to be held a lot.

Resolving a sleep problem

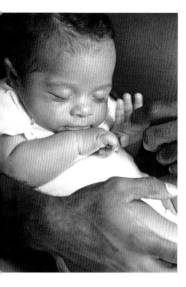

Many people have strong opinions about what causes sleep problems and what you can do about them, often built on personal experience or the experience of friends and relatives. Many parents of babies with sleep problems complain about an over-abundance of advice that can make it difficult for them to work out which particular pieces of advice fit their baby and circumstances. And professionals, too, have differing opinions about appropriate tactics to encourage good sleep habits. This can make a problem even harder for parents to deal with.

This chapter looks first at the best ways to change habits, and then at different ways to teach a baby to fall asleep on his own in the evening or go back to sleep when he wakes during the night.

If your baby has a sleep problem, always start by taking him to the doctor so that any illness can be ruled out, or if present, be treated. Having an illness treated, though, is not always enough to correct the problem. That's because the root of the sleep problem may involve more than just the baby's illness.

Sometimes, the factors that are causing a sleep problem cannot be changed. If you move house frequently, or your baby has an excitable character or even if his new-found motor abilities are disturbing his sleep, you won't be able to do anything much about the causes. But even if this is the case, it will help you to understand what has led to your baby starting to sleep poorly. It's then possible, at least, to respond in an appropriate way.

I have had the most success treating sleep problems when I approach them in the order shown in the box on the opposite page. But it is also possible to work on all three areas at the same time.

The first issue – regulating sleep rhythms – has to be resolved in a way appropriate to your baby's age. Typical timings at different ages are discussed in chapter 4 (see pages 70–131).

As for the second and third issues, it's usually necessary for you to change your responses to your baby's sleep difficulties, or to break habits that you and your baby both have developed, before he can be successfully taught to sleep on his own. Such habits generally consist of particular communication patterns, and you will need to use new ways of responding to your baby when he is put to bed in the evening or when he wakes during the night.

ROUTINES AND HABITS

Habits are ingrained in babies' lives. Having a strict routine and knowing in advance the order in which things happen makes babies feel calm and secure. Babies get used to feeding at particular times and falling asleep in a certain way. You may be happy with an existing routine or you may want to use your baby's liking for order to help create healthy, desirable habits. Examples of these habits include always following the same routine when putting your baby to bed, or always feeding your baby in one particular place and in a particular way.

Sometimes a baby can get stuck in a habit which, in the long run, is definitely less than ideal. A baby may wake up every two to three hours to feed at night even when he no longer needs to as, say, would be the case if he was eight months old and having solids three or four times a day. Babies who were colicky as newborns can sometimes continue to demand extra attention, such as bouncing and rocking, even after their colic is long gone. They are stuck in the habit of being rocked vigorously in order to go to sleep and can't sleep without this assistance.

When you need to change something that your baby is used to, or break a habit, it's often best to do a total about-face in how things are done, instead of trying to change them slowly or little by little. You can, for example, change the place where your baby sleeps, the position of his bed, and what happens before you put him to bed.

BEHAVIOURAL APPROACHES

The most common strategies for resolving sleep problems (apart from problems involving sleep rhythms, see page 42) involve attempts to change a baby's behaviour. This section discusses the main approaches used for babies with sleep problems or other sleep-related issues. The biggest difference between these approaches has to do with how

---

Three-point plan

Correct your baby's sleep timings or rhythms.

Review and change your responses to your baby's waking up at night.

Teach your baby to fall asleep on his own.

"Most babies find it easier to learn new routines than to accept incremental changes in old, well-established habits."

much time you should stay in your baby's physical presence to start with, and how quickly you should move away. At the beginning of the process, do you stay in the same room as your baby or stay outside but come in at regular intervals? The goal of all the approaches is the same: to improve sleep. That usually means teaching your baby to fall asleep on his own and to stop needing assistance to go back to sleep when he wakes during the night.

Behavioural treatment, as the name suggests, attempts to shape or change behaviour. Treatments differ in how strict they are but all have in common that their first step is to create a basic structure for a baby's sleeping habits. This means regular sleep timings, a regular bedtime routine and a regular place where the baby sleeps. Your baby's developmental maturity and temperament should be the key factors in choosing a specific approach. The younger and more sensitive your baby, the more gentle the approach should be. Most experts agree that it's always best to try to choose the gentlest approach possible.

Any 'rules for the timing and length of sleep' depend on your baby's age (see also chapter 4). The various possible methods you can use to teach your baby to fall asleep on his own, whether in the evening or after having woken up at night are described below.

Controlled crying

One of the most widely known approaches in Western countries is 'checking' or 'controlled crying'. This approach is a strict one and in recent years it has become less and less popular. However, it does suit some babies. It works like this: a baby is put to sleep in his bed after a specific bedtime routine. The parent leaves the room immediately, regardless of whether their baby is crying or not. If the baby starts to cry, the parent returns at defined intervals and stays very briefly, for one or two minutes, and then leaves again without fussing too much with their baby. The length of time before going into the baby's room is then increased.

Usually on the first evening the parent starts by going into his or her baby's room after three minutes away. If the baby is still crying, the parent goes in after five minutes, then after seven minutes and step by step up to 15 minutes away. After that, the parent goes into the room every 15 minutes until the baby falls asleep.

The next evening the parent starts by going into the baby's room after five minutes and then after seven minutes, and so on. The intervals are slowly lengthened (as before) until the parent waits 20 minutes before returning to the room. The parent always does the same things when going in to the room, for example, giving the dummy, stroking their baby's head and humming.

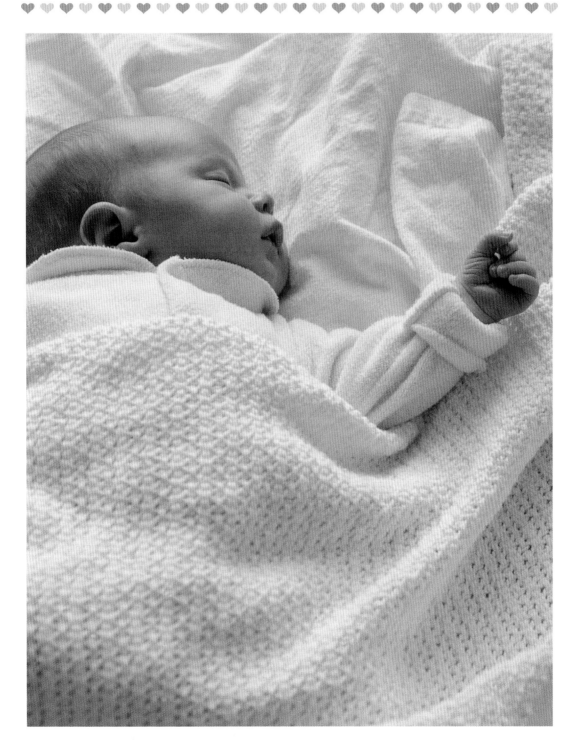

On the third evening, the first return is after seven minutes, and the intervals are again lengthened, as on the previous evenings. How long the parent stays away from the room varies, some don't leave longer than 20 minutes but others wait for longer.

Using this method, parents can proceed according to a rigid, predetermined plan. Many like this, and the method has produced successful results. The main criticism has been that it is used for babies who are too young for such a strict approach – supporters have said that it works for babies as young as five or six months. Critics, myself included, say that letting a small baby cry alone in a room is something that should be evaluated on a case-by-case basis. I do not recommend using this method for babies under the age of 18 months without careful consideration. A good reason to use this method might be if your baby cries more when you are in the room with him than when you are outside – you don't want your presence to make him unhappy.

'Shaping' or 'camping out'

The approach I recommend involves laying a baby in his cot after his bedtime routine, but instead of leaving the room, an adult stays with him from the point when the baby is put in bed until he actually falls asleep. This person sits near the baby (or may lie down), and offers limited assistance, responding in predetermined ways, which depend on the parent's experience of what their child likes (see box on page 63). The parent then reduces the assistance he or she provides day by day, and moves his or her chair further and further from the baby's bed. The main difference between 'controlled crying' and this approach is that the baby is not left crying alone in his room but instead has someone in the room with him and possibly making things easier for him by keeping him company.

It's possible to customise both controlled crying and camping out in a way that you feel is appropriate for yourself and for your baby, but you always need to bear in mind your baby's developmental maturity and how he will experience what you do.

Gradual withdrawal

Most parents who are training a baby to fall asleep on his own find it helpful to think of the process in stages, and I like to speak of the 'step-by-step method' (though many sleep researchers use the term 'gradual withdrawal'). The step-by-step method is a very gentle way to teach babies to fall asleep by themselves. It is appropriate for very young babies (two to three months old) and also for older, sensitive infants. The method has 14 stages or steps during which you very slowly provide less and less assistance to your baby as he goes to sleep.

At stage 1 you are providing maximum assistance, at stage 14, only the bare minimum.

You can decide whether to follow the sequence one step at a time or to skip ahead two or more steps. And if your baby is already ready for, say, step 4, you don't have to start with step 1. Three to four days per step is usually enough to get good results.

If your baby is being breastfed, it's usually better, though not absolutely necessary, for his father (or another carer) to take over after step 4.

For a baby over six months old, you can start with step 9 and work through to step 12.

If your baby is young (under six months) and is determined and strong-willed, it is best not to have too many steps. Babies like this often cry just as much regardless of whether you go slowly or quickly. These babies often find it hard to go one step at a time so it makes sense to take two to three steps at a time up to step 9 or 10.

When you reach step 10 (for all babies), it is good to change your approach a little (see page 61). Go to your baby every few minutes and check up on him in a methodical and businesslike way: hush him softly, make sure he has his dummy (if he uses one) and fix his covers. In between these visits, don't talk to him or offer any service other than the knowledge that you are there. Ideally, act as if you are sleeping or very busy thinking.

The idea is to do less and less, to withdraw slowly from the scene, and to let your baby learn to go to sleep by himself. He needs to work out the most comfortable way to lie and some babies put a lot of effort into trying out different positions.

If you feel that you can't bear comforting your child only every few minutes until he falls asleep (or feel sure you will be in for many hours of crying), you can follow this approach for a limited, predetermined amount of time only. You can use this approach for, say, half an hour (or any other amount of time – shorter periods for younger babies) and if your baby still hasn't calmed down, then you can hold him in your arms, offer him a drink of water and comfort him. But do your best not to take him out of the bedroom, breastfeed or offer him a bottle. And don't turn on the light. Hold him in your arms until he is calm, then try again.

Good sleeping habits depend on

Regular times for sleep.

A regular place to sleep.

Specific bedtime routines.

A systematic approach when attending to the baby.

Stages of reduced assistance

1

The baby is fed outside his bedroom, and then falls asleep and is carried into bed while asleep, or falls asleep in your arms while you walk around. (Either way represents the highest level of service to the baby.)

2

The baby falls asleep while being fed in the bedroom or another area of the home.

3

The baby falls asleep in your arms while being rocked, but not fed.

4

The baby falls asleep in your arms without being rocked.

5

The baby falls asleep in his father's arms.

6

The baby falls asleep next to either parent (both lying in the parental bed) with that parent holding him.

7

The baby falls asleep next to either parent but that parent doesn't hold him.

8

The baby falls asleep next to either parent and that parent turns his or her back to him.

9

The baby falls asleep in his own bed, which is pushed right up against the parental bed, and one parent lies next to the baby, touching him with his or her hand.

10

The baby falls asleep in his own bed with a parent in the parental bed who does not touch him.

11

The baby falls asleep in his own bed with a parent in the parental bed whose back is turned to the baby.

12

The baby falls asleep in his own bed and a parent sits in a chair by his bed.

13

The baby falls asleep in his own bed and a parent sits further away from the bed.

14

The last step is for the parent to leave the room while the baby is falling asleep. There are two good ways to do this. One is to leave the room very briefly each night just after baby is put to bed, and then to come back into the room and stay until the baby has fallen asleep, gradually lengthening the time spent away. The other is to open the door to the baby's room and to occupy yourself conspicuously in front of it (see also pages 46–47).

10

onwards

Whoever doesn't usually put the baby to bed should be the one to train him from step 10 (especially the first three or four nights).

♥

Lie next to the baby or sit in a chair next to his bed (see step 12).

♥

Sit completely still; don't do anything except perhaps a little hushing and humming.

♥

Get up every two to six minutes (depending on your baby's age) and lay him down (if he is sitting up or standing). Give him his dummy or anything else he wants and rearrange his covers.

♥

Sit back down and wait for a few minutes.

♥

Repeat this routine as long as it seems necessary.

♥

If the baby throws all his things out of bed, just let them lie on the floor until the next time you come to him.

♥

Don't make eye contact or talk to or scold your baby. Be as reserved as possible. Some parents and children like to have quiet music on during the process.

TEACHING YOUR BABY TO FALL ASLEEP ON HIS OWN

Your baby will fall asleep more readily on his own if you have set routines and procedures, which are always carried out in the same order and in the same way before sleep. Your baby might, for example, be fed in the living room and then taken into the bedroom. Most commonly, bedtime routines take place in the bedroom before the baby falls asleep, and one goal is to ensure he connects the routine with going to sleep.

The younger the baby, the shorter the routine should be. With a very small baby, you can take him into the bedroom, hold him in your arms while you sing a song and give him a hug, then turn out the light and put him into his cot. When your baby is a little older, you should spend a little longer putting him to bed: you can read a story, say prayers or sing a song, then turn out the light, draw the curtains, put him into his cot and stroke his head.

"The aim of a bedtime routine is to get your baby to accept that, once you have gone through all the stages, it is time to go to sleep."

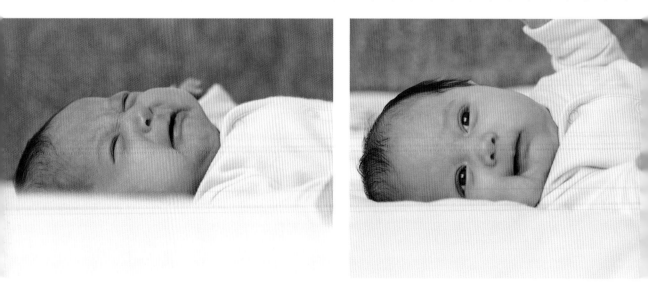

When your baby is even older, you can end the routine by sitting on his bed and talking about something cheerful, so that he falls asleep with pleasant thoughts.

It is important to train your baby to link lying down in one particular place with going to sleep. You should also keep in mind that when your baby wakes up at night, it is logical from his point of view to insist on going back to the place where he fell asleep. He will also want to have the same things done for him when he wakes up during the night as were done when he was originally falling asleep, so you must be prepared to repeat them.

There are various ways to teach a baby to fall asleep on his own. The difference lies in how long you stay in his physical presence at the beginning, what kind of attention he receives during the night, and how quickly this assistance is reduced or withdrawn.

Ways of offering limited assistance

Giving a dummy.

♥

Putting something in the baby's hands.

♥

Stroking the baby's head.

♥

Placing a hand on the baby's tummy and humming, but not looking him in the eye or taking to him.

WHEN YOUR BABY WAKES UP AT NIGHT

Most commonly, babies who wake up at night aren't able to go back to sleep on their own. Some babies fall asleep like angels in the evening, but wake up during the night and start to make all kinds of demands. What you can realistically expect of your baby during the night depends on his age. (There are more detailed descriptions of the approaches and strategies you can use in chapter 4.)

When dealing with night-time waking, the first thing to look at is whether the timings of your baby's daytime naps are OK. A common reason for waking up at night is that a baby waits too long before taking his daytime nap. The next thing to look at is if your baby needs assistance to fall asleep in the evening. If there is no problem with either of these issues, then the next step is to review how you respond when your baby wakes up.

What to do when your baby wakes up

You can help your baby to get back to sleep during the night by gradually doing less and less to help him:

Decide which parent (or other carer) will respond to the baby (as he or she will be the only one sleeping in the baby's room). Bear in mind that a baby who wakes at night will want the same conditions that he experienced just before going to sleep in the evening.

When the baby wakes up, wait a little – about two to four minutes if he is five to six months old (and longer if he is older, regardless of what he is doing, such as standing up or banging on his cot bars). Don't respond to him too quickly. The carer should get up and lay the baby back down (if he is sitting up or standing). Give him his dummy or anything else he wants. Finally, put his comfort item next to him or in his hand. Then lie down and wait for a few minutes. Repeat the above as often as necessary.

If the baby throws things out of the bed on to the floor, don't pick them up until you next tend to him.

Don't look the baby in the eye, don't chat with him and don't scold him – it's best to be as neutral as possible.

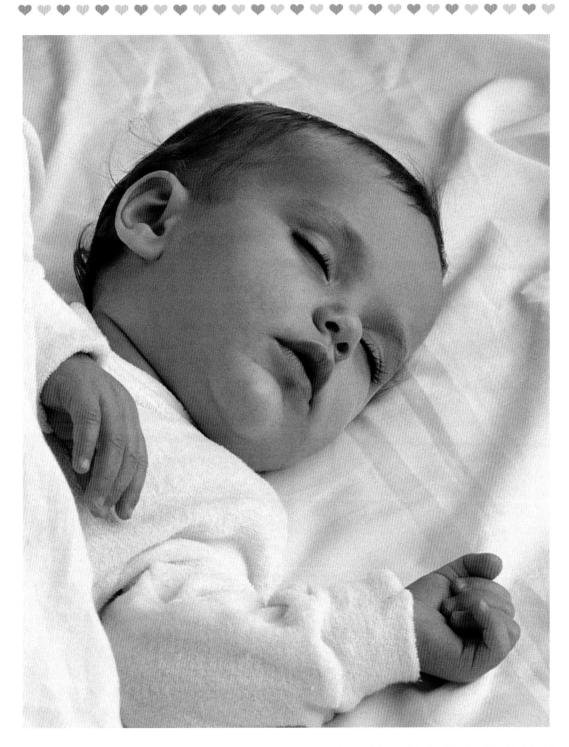

FALLING ASLEEP ON HIS OWN IN THE DAYTIME

If you want to teach your baby to fall asleep on his own, you should slowly and with as little fuss as possible, start with nap time, only later tackling bedtime in the evening. Ideally, begin with the first nap of the day, before noon. At this time of day your baby will be at his most receptive, and training him is more likely to go smoothly and succeed. Babies who need help falling asleep during the daytime more often take shorter naps than babies who can fall asleep on their own. These shorter naps often last only 30 to 45 minutes.

You can make a step-by-step plan just as you would for night (see the example on pages 60–61) when trying to help your baby fall asleep alone for his naps.

If there is more than one child in the household day and night are usually clearly defined: the activity level in the home becomes a marker of day and night. But a parent who is alone at home with a baby needs to think about how to do this. Turning on a light or the radio, or opening the curtains, communicates to your baby that it's day now. Some parents like to have their baby nap in a pram (either indoors or out, as circumstances dictate). A pram enables you to be somewhere other than at home while your baby naps. The goal is to be able to lay your baby down to sleep while he is fully awake and for him to then fall asleep peacefully on his own. The first nap of the day is usually the best time to let a baby fall asleep on his own. That also means that the first nap is when you can wait the longest before starting to rock your baby or pushing his pram. With later naps, you can wait less. Any rocking or pushing should be no more vigorous than necessary (see box above).

"It's good if your baby's daytime sleeping environment is a little different from his night-time surroundings."

Teaching a baby to fall asleep on his own for daytime naps

As with everything else, babies learn by repetition and you can help him to fall asleep for a daytime nap:

✓ Decide on a regular time for the nap (depending on your baby's age) and where he will sleep during the day.

✓ Make sure that his daytime sleep environment is a little different from his night-time surroundings. This is often important when training a baby to fall asleep on his own, but no longer an issue once he starts sleeping well.

✓ When getting him ready for a nap, follow the same routine every day; for example, hum a particular tune while arranging him in bed or in the pram.

✓ Put him to sleep with his dummy (if he uses one). It's also a good idea to put something in or by his hand; babies like to have something to hold or fiddle with.

✓ At first, just stay with him quietly; don't rock him or push his pram. If he starts to cry, wait for one or two minutes. Give him a dummy or other comfort item. Then sit quietly again. Repeat this process several times (the older the baby, the more often it can be repeated), hopefully until he falls asleep. If your baby is very young, or if you expect a lot of resistance, decide in advance to follow this approach only for a set number of minutes and, if your baby doesn't fall asleep within this time, start rocking him or pushing his pram until he falls asleep. Do this as gently as possible.

✓ If your baby still won't fall asleep, it's time for a break. Take him out of bed or the pram and let him calm down completely for 10–20 minutes. Then put him back to sleep, in the same way, repeating all the same steps. Don't use any of the methods that you are trying to discontinue (like feeding him or carrying him around in your arms).

SLEEP PROBLEMS RELATING TO FEEDING

Parents sometimes ask whether, as their baby approaches his first birthday, they really ought to stop letting him fall asleep while drinking from his bottle if he is already sleeping well all night. The answer is that there is no reason to do this with any great fanfare, but you should keep in mind that there is a certain risk involved in a baby falling asleep while feeding. If, for example, the baby is ill or out of sorts in some other way, there is a chance that he could start to wake up at night and ask for conditions to revert to those in which he fell asleep. (See also page 138 on illness and sleep routines.)

It's possible to step down evening bottlefeeds slowly by filling the bottle less and less full or progressively thin it down with water (see page 111). It also helps to give your baby porridge (see page 41) before his evening bottle so he drinks less milk. Water before sleep, which is better for his teeth, is a more suitable alternative before he goes to sleep for the night.

For a six- to 12-month-old baby who falls asleep on the breast, you should breastfeed him an hour to an hour and a half before bedtime, then give him porridge just before sleep, and offer the breast again. He is likely not to want to drink much, and will be less prone to fall asleep while feeding.

You have a six-month-old baby who is used to falling asleep on his mother's breast in the living room…

…To change this situation you can do the following. First, put Daddy in charge of putting him to bed. In order to make this less stressful for your baby, you should disappear from the scene (even leave the house) 15 to 30 minutes before bedtime, after you have fed the baby (it is okay to breastfeed him a little earlier than usual). With you out of sight, your baby is less likely to cry for your attention. Dad should create a definite but simple bedtime routine. For example, after you have fed your baby and left, Dad takes the baby into the bedroom, closes the curtains, turns off the lights, and holding him in his arms, sings a lullaby before putting him into his cot. All this happens in the same order every evening.

In this scenario, your baby is no longer permitted to fall asleep on his mother in the living room, but instead is put to bed in the bedroom. Later, you can choose how your baby will be taught to fall asleep (see pages 62).

Your 12-month-old baby is used to having his bottle filled three times a night but is able to fall asleep on his own in the evening…

…You can make the following changes. First, you need to change where your baby sleeps: move his bed to another room or to another area in the same room. By changing his environment, you will make it easier for him to accept a change in routine at the same time. Babies are often more at ease with learning new things in a new context.

Then you need to change his usual night-time carer. The parent (or a relative or friend) who does not normally look after him at night takes over these duties. This new person should put him to bed – even if your baby can fall asleep on his own – so he won't be surprised if this person comes to him during the night. This new carer should start by sleeping in the same room as your baby.

When your baby wakes up at night, the new carer should respond in a totally new way. Note that it isn't possible to teach a child of this age, who is used to having so much to drink, to be happy with just one bottle a night: you have to stop all night-time feeds. You need to decide in advance how the carer will act. A simple and determined way is when your baby wakes and starts to cry, the carer should wait for three to five minutes before responding, then go to him and lay him down without picking him up, give him his dummy and cuddly toy, then stroke him for a few moments.

In this scenario, the bottle plays the leading role in the drama, and making it disappear is the best way to break the habit. To break the bottle habit, you need to make sure your baby cannot lay eyes on a bottle at all for some time – not even on the shelf or in other babies' hands. You won't stop giving him milk during the day – he needs it for his calcium intake – but from now on he should be given his milk in a cup.

If your baby is used to feeding so much during the night, you also need to ensure that he is going to bed with a full tummy. Feed him solids twice during the evening before he goes to sleep, for example dinner at 6 and a snack at 8 p.m. If you are worried that he is not getting enough to drink, you should offer him extra milk from a cup at 7 p.m. in your arms.

Your baby's sleep at different ages

The following chapter discusses how you can realistically expect your baby to sleep, at different ages and levels of maturity. If your baby sleeps in a different way from those discussed here, and sleeps well, then you should not change her sleep patterns. Like other books about bringing up children, mine is designed to support you as a parent, and you shouldn't take its advice as the only right way to do things. Remember, you and your baby are unique and there is no one-size-fits-all situation!

Newborn

Most healthy, full-term newborns sleep for long stretches, which are evenly distributed throughout the day and night. The majority wake up briefly when they are fed and then sleep in between. It's best to think of your baby's first days and weeks of life as an adjustment period – to new sleeping and feeding habits, and to a separate existence in general. If you try to put yourself in your newborn's place, you can see that she has gone through a tremendous change so it's best to make her first experiences with life as peaceful as possible. It's good to have the lights dim and the noise level low, and to keep movements calm when handling her. A tiny baby also needs lots of warmth and human company. Providing a tranquil environment helps this newly born individual to feel comfortable and sleep well.

A sleeping newborn spends a lot of time in light sleep, as if drowsing in between slumber and wakefulness. If your baby starts to cry under these conditions, you may start to think that she is waking up and tend to her unnecessarily. It's always good to wait for a moment (for example, by counting to ten) before intervening and comforting her, just to see whether she is really waking up or just murmuring and stretching in her sleep.

ENCOURAGING GOOD SLEEPING HABITS

Some babies, but by no means all, start to sleep longer at night and stay awake more during the day completely on their own. Most develop good habits in some areas and not in others. For example, a baby may start to fall asleep easily at night, but not during the day, or vice versa. If you follow some simple guidelines from the start, however, your baby can learn good sleeping habits and ultimately sleep well. Babies like habit and routine, and feel calm and secure when things are proceeding according to plan. In order to reinforce this, it makes good sense to create healthy routines for your baby from the start.

"Babies are by nature creatures of habit, and feel calm and secure when things happen according to plan."

Good sleeping habits from the start

Evidence shows that the following four factors promote good sleeping habits:

1 Teaching your baby the difference between day and night.

2 Preserving your baby's ability to fall asleep without help.

3 Setting regular feeding and sleeping times.

4 Choosing one night-time sleep period and working to lengthen it without feeding.

The difference between day and night

Try to help your baby to discriminate between day and night from the start. A reasonable approach is to make the hours between midnight and 7 or 8 a.m. 'night-time'. Night-time means that it's dark (or there's a minimum of light) and that no-one talks very much. During night-time, you only provide necessary services, such as giving your baby something to drink and changing her nappy, if necessary. (Try to do this without turning on the light or putting the baby on the changing table.) And when you give this care, you carry it out with as little light and communication as possible. You want to give your baby the message that this is the time for snuggling up and trying to get back to sleep as soon as possible – night is a time for calm and quiet.

Falling asleep without help

Babies are born with the ability to fall asleep on their own, or 'self-soothe' as it is sometimes called. There are two things you need to do to make sure this ability is not lost: you should give your baby sufficient time to fall asleep on her own, and you should ensure your baby has a regular place or places to sleep.

Your newborn will often – and unavoidably – fall asleep while feeding, but it's possible to prevent this from happening every single time if you are diligent and sometimes put your baby to bed while awake and let her fall asleep undisturbed. In this way, she will learn gently that sleeping and feeding are not inextricably linked. Bear in mind that most babies have an easier time falling asleep on their own early in the day and need more assistance as it gets later. It's also good to avoid feeding your baby in a position in which she is likely to fall asleep in the process. Try sitting upright with your baby in your arms rather than feeding her while lying down, for example.

Some tummy time

Babies who cry a lot or are 'colicky' often don't want to lie on their back. They want to be on their tummy, as they feel more comfortable that way. If your baby cries a lot or has colic (see page 86), lay her on her side and support her tummy with a rolled-up blanket placed against it. Then stretch her lower arm (the one next to the mattress) out slightly, perpendicular to her body. This will keep her from rolling completely on to her tummy.

Don't let your baby spend all her time lying on her back, as there's a danger that her back, neck and shoulder muscles won't get the training that they need, and that the back of her head will get too flat. Let her play on her tummy when she is awake and with you. It's important to start doing this right away, otherwise she might start to dislike lying on her tummy. A good way to start practising is by letting her lie face downwards on your chest. Similarly, when she has just woken up and is up for a little bit of exercise, you can put her on a flat and not too soft surface like a yoga mat or rug.

You can, if you like, put some simple black and white illustrations in front of her or to her side to encourage her to lift her head up and look around.

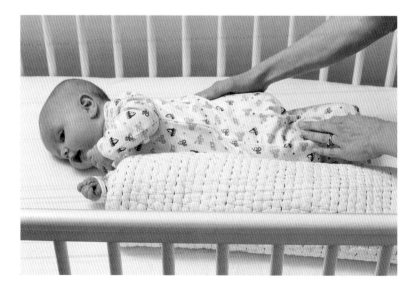

It's also important that your baby learns that going to sleep happens in a particular place – that means that she lies down, still awake, in the same place in order to fall asleep. That said, it's not ideal to let her fall asleep in a room where there are all sorts of noises and distractions. While it's all right if this happens every now and then, it ought to be the exception rather than the rule. There's no reason to isolate a baby from normal household sounds (like conversation or the radio, or the noise of appliances like the washing machine) while she is falling asleep, but avoid turning on a light or the television in the room where she sleeps. If space is limited and she has to share a bedroom, put her cot in one corner of the room (always the same one) and keep any light sources from shining on her.

Your baby doesn't need to sleep in the same bed or place during the day and at night. Many parents like to have a cot for the night and use a Moses basket or cradle for daytime naps, and have their baby nearby (say, in a corner of the kitchen, living room or study).

"Babies can be great at falling asleep on their own during the first weeks of life and then start to have more and more trouble."

Many babies fall asleep easily on their own during the first weeks of life and then start to have more trouble. Their inborn ability can, so to speak, be disturbed, and the reasons for this vary. The most common causes are that parents respond too quickly to their baby (immediately running to care for her at any sign of wakefulness) or that a baby feels pain or discomfort of some sort, for example, due to what is usually called colic. On page 44, I discuss how to teach a baby to develop the ability to fall asleep on her own after having lost the initial skill.

Back to sleep and SIDS

In the 1980s, health professionals in many countries started to recommend putting babies to sleep on their back. The reason was that a link had been found between SIDS (sudden infant death syndrome, or cot death) and babies sleeping on their tummy. Today, parents all over the world are told that babies should sleep on their back, both at night and for daytime naps.

In cot death, an apparently healthy baby under one year of age dies without any visible explanation. SIDS is one of the worst fears for parents; when it happens, it is terrifying and indescribably sorrowful. SIDS is most common between the ages of two and four months. It almost never occurs during a newborn's first weeks.

Despite many extensive studies of its cause, no-one has yet managed to explain exactly why or how it happens. We do know that smoking during pregnancy or around a baby is a risk factor while breastfeeding and letting a newborn sleep with a dummy seem to have a protective effect. We don't know why these latter things reduce the risk, but it's likely that they combine with many other factors that are still obscure. Fortunately, SIDS is very rare. By following the dos and don'ts (see right), you can reduce its likelihood even further, although you cannot eliminate it entirely.

Set regular feeding and sleeping times

For newborns, feeding and sleeping are connected, which is why there is a link between regular feeding times and regular sleeping times. A baby who, for example, drinks quite often but never takes very much at a time is also likely to want to sleep frequently but never for very long. If your baby is like this, you may want to lengthen the daytime naps she takes, and it's easiest to do so by lengthening the time between feeds.

If you need to make sleeping times more regular, it's good to make feeding times more regular too. Ideally, you want feeding habits to help improve sleeping habits. When trying to make a small baby's feeding times more regular, a realistic approach is to leave more time

Do

✓ Put your baby to sleep on her back. Place her feet at the foot of the cot so she can't wriggle under the covers.

✓ Make sure she cannot get too warm while she is sleeping (use several lightweight blankets rather than one heavy one).

✓ Have her sleep in a separate cot or cradle in your room for the first months.

✓ Breastfeed her, if at all possible.

✓ Let her sleep with a dummy.

✓ Take her to the doctor if you have any reason to think she is ill.

Don't

✗ Smoke in pregnancy, let anyone smoke near your baby or in your home.

✗ Let her sleep with a pillow or anything soft and heavy (like a duvet), which she can pull over her head.

✗ Make the bedroom too warm: the optimum temperature is around 16–20°C (61–68°F).

✗ Fit a bumper around the cot; this can prevent air from circulating and cause the baby to overheat.

between feeds early in the day and less time between those later in the day. As the day goes on, your baby is more awake, her digestion works faster, and she needs to feed more often. You can expect your baby to be able to go three to four hours between feeds early in the day but only two to three hours later in the day. If your baby is used to feeding more often, take things slowly; wait two to three hours between feeds in the morning and one to two hours later in the day.

Choosing one night-time sleep period

Your baby will stop night-time feeds earlier if you work slowly and deliberately, from the beginning, to lengthen one of her periods of sleep. Note that you should only try this if your baby weighs at least 3 kilos, or 6½ pounds. Also, though I say 'from the beginning', you should wait until your baby is one to three weeks old before starting.

For a newborn, night typically starts around midnight. The goal is then to make the period before the first night feed as long as possible. Realistically, you can expect this time to be about three hours to start with, and then to get slowly longer, for example from midnight to 3:30 a.m., then to 4 a.m., and so on (30 minutes being an appropriate time span). If you started at one week of age, your baby could be sleeping five hours in the first stretch of the night at six weeks. Some babies stop feeding at night very quickly, while others need encouragement and assistance to go longer between feeds. If your baby has trouble holding out until her next feed, she may find it easier if someone other than her mother tends to her in between. This is especially true for breastfed babies, who may not be happy with Mummy's help unless it comes with her breast as well.

"A newborn will sleep for about three hours without a feed and should be able to go for five hours by about six weeks of age."

Should my month-old baby have a regular sleeping routine?

My son is a month old and I am wondering whether I can do something to help him sleep better, or whether he is still too young. He sleeps at very irregular times of the day and night. He does, though, usually fall asleep between 2 and 3 a.m. and wakes up around 6 a.m. Then I breastfeed him and he falls asleep again, and sleeps for another 2–2½ hours. Then it varies how long he sleeps during the day. Usually he stays awake for an hour and then sleeps for between 15 and 60 minutes at a time. He almost always falls asleep while breastfeeding. He isn't a difficult baby at all – he's really easy – although in the evenings, he doesn't like it when his father spends too much time with him; he's happiest around me then.

I've been told I should breastfeed him whenever he wants, and he wants to very frequently. He is almost constantly on my breast in the evenings and all the way up to 2 a.m. when he finally falls asleep. He nods off every now and then in the evenings, just in my arms. This is really cosy for both of us, but we're wondering whether it might be possible to get him to fall asleep a little earlier – at least around midnight. He is our first child and I'm told that little by little he'll learn to sleep all night and he'll start to breastfeed more regularly. Is that true?

ARNA'S ANSWER

There are various things you can do to build a foundation for good sleeping habits. With such a little baby you have to do everything slowly. Watch the direction his sleeping habits are moving in and encourage any positive trends. What you've been told is true; some babies sleep better as they get older, and how much help babies need to sleep well varies a lot. I'm going to go over a few things here, which you can then put to work at your own speed. You say he is an easy baby, which means it's more likely that you can help him form good habits without a lot of protest.

Feeding: The first thing I think you should look at is your breastfeeding routine. You said that you had been told to 'breastfeed whenever he wants'. In fact, you should breastfeed him whenever he needs but sometimes it can be a little hard to work out when a baby needs to feed. The risk is that your baby will start to get fed every time he cries, or almost every time – and he may be crying for many reasons other than hunger. He also could start to use you as a dummy (see also page 48).

A baby needs to feed more often in the latter part of the day and the evening in order to be full for the night, but it isn't ideal to have a baby constantly on the breast in the evenings as you describe. What you say about it feeling cosy to have a newborn in your arms is totally true. Few things are cosier. A baby needs closeness and contact, but doesn't always need to feed. So, hold him in your arms but enforce some minimum time – say, an hour to begin with – between feeds. You didn't say how long he feeds, but with some babies, breastfeeding sessions run together, so that the baby starts spending a long time drinking. If this is the case with your baby, you will have to ration the time that he is allowed to drink. Babies quickly learn to concentrate and so drink faster. This advice may seem a little at odds with what you've been told, but hopefully it's not too confusing. Conflicting advice about caring for a baby is hard for new parents. The fact is that there are just different opinions about how to handle breastfeeding babies. Parents need to choose what suits their family best.

Falling asleep: You say he always falls asleep while breastfeeding. You need to train him to fall asleep on his own and it's best to do this slowly. He is probably – like most babies – calmest in the morning. Use his first nap of the day as practice for falling asleep on his own. Lay him down in his cradle, sit calmly

next to him and touch him. If he can't settle down, hush him and pat his back lightly. Sometimes this will work and sometimes it won't, but try it twice a day in the morning. It should start to work better and better. If he protests, try an even softer method, where he falls asleep on your chest (but not while breastfeeding) and then on his father's chest. Then you can let him fall asleep lying next to you, with less and less hushing and patting. In this way, you step down the level of attention and assistance while he is falling asleep (see also page 63).

Sleep timings: Keep a sleep diary for a few days so you can see whether he manages to settle into a regular routine, like when he wakes up in the morning or when he takes a nap during the day. The goal here is to get your son's body clock into a pattern. It's good to set a specific time for when he will wake up in the morning. You could, for example, wake him up at 9 a.m. (it makes sense to choose the time when he most often wakes up now, or a little before that time). Then he should stay awake for an hour or a little more – that's probably about the amount of time he can manage at the moment. Then he can take his first nap. Don't try to fix all his sleep and waking times in one go. Keep in mind that his ability

to stay awake increases as the day progresses. That means that he will stay awake longer and longer between naps as the day goes on. Try to fix three specific times for him: the time that he falls asleep in the evening, the time he wakes up in the morning and the time that he takes his first nap.

Night: Your baby dozes a lot in the evenings while breastfeeding, and though this is cosy now it is not ideal in the long run. Try to create at least some basic routine for breastfeeding: irregular feeding often leads to irregular sleeping! Let his father look after him a little in the evenings, even if your baby complains about this a little – the two of them will be able to work it out. Indeed, this will be good for their relationship (you should go out for a walk or take a bath while they're together). It would be good if your little boy could stay awake for a couple of hours before he goes to sleep for the night (that means being wide awake, without feeding, except just before he goes to sleep). Start by keeping your night-time routine the same as it is now, but start it at 2 a.m. rather than 3 a.m. Then move it earlier by 30 minutes every three to four days. When you've got to midnight or 11 p.m., stay put for a little while (one or two weeks) and then start moving his bedtime earlier again.

Two to four months

Parents often wonder how many hours a baby should sleep each day. For babies aged under three months, the answer can vary a lot because there are wider individual differences between their sleeping habits and those of older babies. Moreover, many young babies spend a lot of time in a drowsy, half-asleep state, which is often not counted as sleep time. To make things even more confusing, babies can make quite a bit of noise while 'sleeping' in this way.

TWO MONTHS OLD

It's realistic to expect that, at around two months of age, your baby's night-time sleep will last about eight hours. With such a young baby, though, it may not be clear when the night begins and ends. Your baby may, for example, like to wake up two or three times during the night to feed during these eight hours so that, instead of leaping bright-eyed out of bed at 7 a.m. to start the day, you'll do anything you can to sleep a little longer, even just for a few minutes. You may, therefore, choose to stay in bed to feed (particularly if you are breastfeeding), which can result in your baby spending much of the early morning on the breast and it will be very unclear to him when the day begins. Or your baby might wake up at 7 or 8 a.m., stay awake for 20 to 30 minutes, and then fall asleep again until mid-morning. That makes the day start for him around 10 a.m., because those 20 to 30 minutes earlier in the morning are too little to give him the feeling that the day has started. Both of these situations can lead to later and later evening bedtimes and very irregular daytime naps.

Your baby needs clear signals about when the day begins, for example, when the lights are turned on and/or the curtains opened, and when people start to talk together, move about and leave the bedroom. I advise mothers to get up with a bound and start the day in a very conspicuous way, but you also need to take care to get enough sleep yourself.

A good strategy if you are tired, is to lie down at the same time as your baby takes his first nap of the day. This is the best time of the day for you to catch up on sleep as it's usually the calmest time of the day. Sleeping in the afternoon is more likely to disturb the following night's sleep.

Typical sleep and wake times for a two-month-old baby

This baby sleeps for five hours at night before getting up to feed at around 4:30 a.m. He then falls back to sleep for another two hours then wakes and feeds again. He sleeps for another hour until 8 a.m., when his day starts.

It's realistic to expect a baby to spend 1–1½ hours awake before taking his first nap. He should then be put to bed for a nap in some place other than where he sleeps at night. If he sleeps in the same bed both at night and during the day, you need to make some kind of change in the surroundings in order to create a distinct 'daytime nap' feeling: a little light or the radio could be turned on, baby could be laid down facing in the opposite direction, or be covered by a blanket instead of being changed into a sleepsuit. Then, as the day progresses, he will stay awake longer and longer between naps – the longest time awake will be just before going to sleep for the night, when he should be able to stay awake for 2–2½ hours. Longer naps early in the day and shorter ones later on help night-time sleeping.

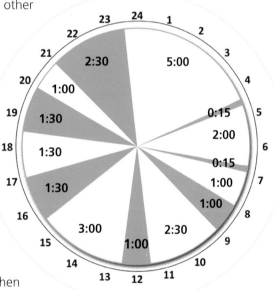

Comforting a crying or colicky baby

Your baby's cries will affect you greatly and elicit all kinds of responses, directed at getting your baby to stop crying. Bear in mind that crying is a precursor to speech so you should practise 'reading' your baby's cry although it is much easier to interpret some cries than others.

There are many kinds of crying, and your baby will cry in very different ways depending on what he is trying to communicate. He also can cry differently for different audiences – for example, more piteously when you are there. He might be playing with his grandmother, totally cheerfully, and then you come home and he starts to bawl, as if something terrible is happening when, in fact, your baby is just saying, 'It's so good to see you.' Some babies tend to the melodramatic, others are quick to start sobbing, and so on. All these factors play into the effect that crying has on you.

Why does a baby cry? The first things that should occur to you when your baby cries is that he is either ill or hungry. It's important to rule out illness as a cause of crying. This is especially important if your baby's cry is different from usual, with a change in tone, or if he cries in circumstances that don't usually trouble him. Babies can cry for many other reasons than illness or hunger; sometimes the answer is obvious and it's very clear how to respond.

If your baby is always fed when he cries, you risk that he will learn that having something to drink is the main avenue of comfort for crying, regardless of whether he is hungry. You will

Dim the lights and reduce any noise then sit with your baby in your arms, skin to skin with his chest against yours and covered by a blanket. Just sit calmly and, at most, hush him or hum to him or talk quietly and tap a gentle, tranquil rhythm with your palm on his back (make sure to keep it very light and peaceful). Don't rock him, walk around with him or bounce him.

then have a harder time learning what his crying actually means. And if he is breastfeeding, he will start to regard your breast as a dummy. Being seen as a dummy is not an appealing fate over the long term, not least because your baby understandably wants control over when he gets his dummy.

What to try

There are many ways to comfort your baby other than by feeding him, but what suits individual babies and individual circumstances varies. Many babies, but by no means all, want to be swaddled and held close. Some babies, including those who are sensitive to any kind of stimulation, are not happy about being held too tightly; very lively babies have no patience for being restrained in any way. When a baby like this puts on a dramatic crying show, it's often good to lay him down on something soft (a bed or sofa), dim the lights, hold one toy within his view and hush him or hum to him. You shouldn't touch him or talk to him – just reduce all stimuli, but keep one toy or picture in view that he can look at.

The best method of comforting a very young baby is usually to sit somewhere calm with him in your arms and hum to him.

White noise, like running water, a fan or a vacuum cleaner, is often used instead of humming to comfort small babies. Be careful not to overuse white noise, however, as your baby may start to want it on all the time. It's best to use sounds that are low in tone.

Some babies may demand much more stimulation than I have recommended using. They often want someone to dance them around the house, bouncing them up and down all the way. But if your baby seems to want more stimulation, you always should do as little as possible in the way of bouncing, rocking and other movements. Rocking and bouncing do comfort a baby for the moment, but the danger is that it will stress him and he may then demand to be bounced more and more often. The main goal in comforting a baby should be to calm him, not to make him stop crying as soon as possible.

COLIC

If your baby won't stop crying, it's essential to take him to the doctor for a thorough check-up, as illness could be the root cause of his cries. If, as with most young babies who cry a lot, no clear explanation can be found, your baby may be said to have 'colic'.

What this means varies although it always includes that your baby cries a lot. Some colicky babies cry most at particular times of the day, often later in the day or in the early part of the night, and frequently for a fairly definite length of time, such as from 8 p.m. to 2 a.m. Other babies don't limit their crying to particular times – they cry more or less all the time.

We don't know for sure what causes this prodigious crying. There are all kinds of possible explanations, but the most likely one is some kind of delayed development, perhaps in the digestive tract or in the perception and processing of various stimuli. It's clear that some colicky babies feel stomach pain – they contract their stomach muscles and screw up their tummies. These are often the babies who cry at particular times of the day. The ones who are sensitive to stimuli, in contrast, are more often those who are ill at ease every now and then around the clock.

The symptoms of colic disappear in most babies by three to five months of age, which suggests that the cause is indeed developmental, and resolves itself with increased maturity as the baby grows older.

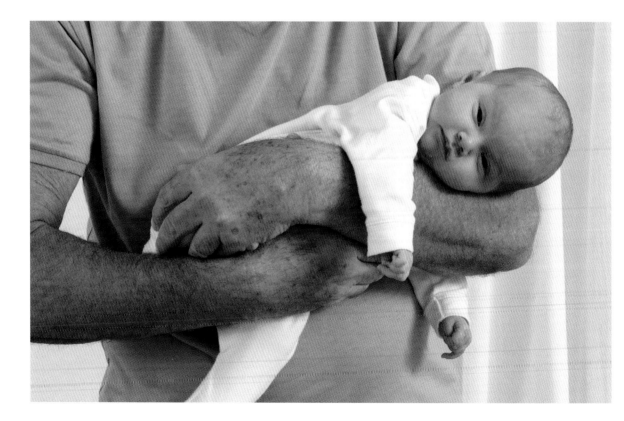

What to try

It can be difficult to comfort a colicky baby. Successful comforting often involves lots of stimulation – rocking, bouncing and other kinds of commotion. Never forget, however, to try to keep the stimulation level to a minimum. Some babies can demand a lot of movement and motion even though it doesn't actually help them. They don't realise that although being bounced around settles them down for the moment, it ultimately prolongs their discomfort. Always try to comfort your baby as peacefully as possible.

Also avoid constantly feeding your colicky baby while he is uncomfortable (many colicky babies want to feed in frequent small amounts during the hours when their colic is acting up). If you do so and are bottlefeeding, your baby can consume a lot of milk which may make him sick, with the result that he feels even worse. If you are breastfeeding, the danger is that your baby can start to drink too much so-called foremilk. Foremilk, which is sugary, is what your baby gets first when he breastfeeds; hind milk, which comes later in a breastfeed, contains more fat. Because of its sweetness, foremilk can make an upset stomach worse.

It's best to feed your baby at the end of his colicky time, once he stops crying. However, what comforts a colicky baby varies from individual to individual, as the causes of colic are so unclear. You may need to experiment to see what works best for you and your baby.

When caring for a baby who is very fretful and cries a lot, the most important thing of all is to involve other people in his care. If your baby is very restless, you will inevitably become totally exhausted, especially if your baby cries a lot at night. No-one can stay awake all day and all night for very long. Your baby's crying will make you feel inadequate and helpless.

Although it does pass, it is a very tough stage of life to get through. You may need a long time to regain your energy levels after your baby's colic improves. Like all parents, you will be preoccupied with doing a good job and showing that you can care for your child. This is important for your self-image. You may find it hard asking for or accepting help. When, on top of this, you are tired and short of sleep, your confidence can plummet. It then gets even harder to ask for help.

If your baby cries a lot, you need to realise that good parenting in such situations means building up a support network for yourself and your baby during these first months. That's the proper response to the problems that your family is experiencing. Sometimes, you may need a lot of self-assurance to be able to accept help.

Support from family and friends is what you need above all else. And the people helping out need to understand that their main role is to support you and make it easier to care for your baby, not to offer advice unless it's asked for. Their role should be to look after your baby for an hour or two at a time, to give you a chance to marshall your energy reserves.

"Your baby should grow out of the need for a midnight feed around the age of four months."

Midnight feeds

If your very young baby (under three months of age) starts to go to sleep for the night at an early hour of the evening, I recommend a 'midnight feed', that is, you feed your baby before you go to bed. For example, if your baby goes to bed for the night at 8 or 9 p.m., before you go to sleep (say at 11 p.m. or midnight), you should take him in your arms, feed him without waking him and gently put him back down in his cot when he has had enough. This is a good approach to take with a baby who is relatively easy (not waking up at night more than would be expected) and has just started to fall asleep early in the evening. Without a late-night feed, your baby is likely to wake up

Two-and-a-half-month-old baby who falls asleep in the early evening

This baby falls asleep just past 8 p.m., and is fed (without being awoken) at 11 p.m. At 4 a.m. he wakes up and is allowed to feed again. Then he falls back asleep and wakes up at 6:30 a.m. ready to start the day. He has a 2-hour nap from 8 to 10 a.m., a 3½-hour nap at 11:30 a.m. to 3 p.m., and finally a quick ½-hour snooze from 5 to 5:30 p.m.

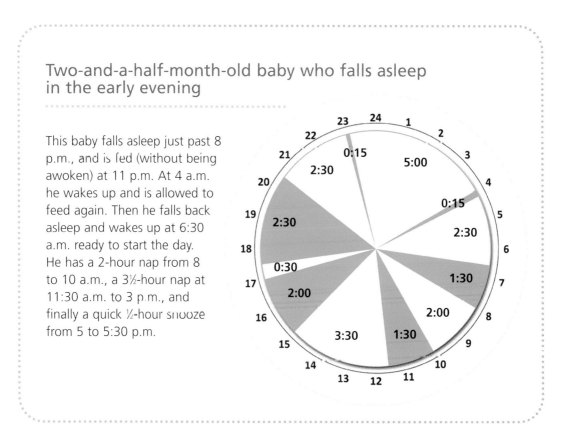

hungry shortly thereafter anyway, as he is too young to go without food for such a long time.

On the other hand, midnight feeds are not a good approach for (say) a five-month-old baby who has, for some reason, just recently jumped from two night-time feeds (at 3 and 5 a.m.) up to four (at 12, 2, 4, and 6 a.m., for example) as some children tend to do at this age. In such a case, it doesn't normally make sense to try to keep the midnight feed while discontinuing all the others. What works for a two- or three-month-old baby can be much too complicated for a five-month-old, who will have a much more definite opinion than a younger baby of the arrangements being made on his behalf.

When, though, will a baby grow out of the need for midnight feeds? Ideally, at around the age of four to five months he will show less and less interest in them. It's good, then, to avoid encouraging your baby to feed at midnight and instead to let him drink less and less (timing the feed if you are breastfeeding or giving less and less in the bottle). Next, try to skip the midnight feed every now and then and see how long your baby can stay asleep without it.

THREE TO FOUR MONTHS OLD

By the time your baby is three to four months old, his sleeping pattern should become more regular. Typically, he might sleep for nine to 10 hours at night and wake up for one or two feeds during that time. Then he will need to be awake for about an hour and a half during the morning in order to feel that the day has definitely started. Most babies at this age take three daytime naps though the length of these naps varies a lot from baby to baby. Your baby might take one long nap and two short ones, or three naps of more or less equal length. Ideally, the longest time awake should be just before bedtime; the last nap of the day should be the shortest, and should get shorter and shorter over time until eventually it is dropped completely.

For a baby of this age, a night-time feed should be as late as possible – say around 5 a.m. Moreover, the last nap of the day should be shortened so that a baby wakes up at 6:30 p.m., and can then be put to bed for the night a little earlier. Babies often adopt to such a schedule on their own, but it's good to know what kind of changes will promote and support them doing so. For example, it is good to encourage a baby to stay awake longer in the morning, by not letting him fall back to sleep immediately after the 7 a.m. feed and for him to take a shorter final nap in the afternoon. Otherwise, you risk increasing the night-time feeds from one to two, and even three (or more), and your baby would go to sleep later and later in the evening.

Typical sleep and wake times for a three-month-old baby

This baby goes to sleep at 10 p.m. and sleeps until 4 a.m. when he wakes up to feed and then sleeps on until a little after 7 a.m. Then it's daytime, and he stays awake for 1½ hours. He then takes two solid naps and one shorter nap. The first nap lasts from about 9 to a little after 11 a.m. (2¼ hours) The second runs from roughly 1 to 3 p.m. (2 hours). The third nap starts at 5:30 p.m. and lasts 1–1½ hours. This baby then stays awake from 7 to 10 p.m.

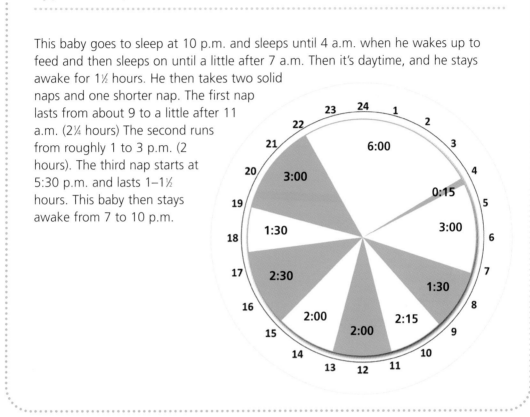

DEVELOPMENTAL FACTORS AFFECTING SLEEP

A baby's self-image starts developing right from birth. Your baby perceives himself at first as a part of you, his mother. Like most babies, your baby then learns to distinguish himself from you without you being aware of the process. Your baby slowly starts to perceive that he is one individual and you are another. However, it can take some time for babies who spend a lot of time with their mothers to make this distinction. If your baby goes for a long time before understanding it, he may start to act very selfishly towards you, as if you are supposed to do exactly what he wants. To help your baby learn this lesson, the most important thing is to get others involved in his care. To start with, your baby should have two principal carers, most commonly his two parents. Then more and more individuals should gradually be added in order to broaden the circle of people who the baby trusts and permits to help with his daily routines.

TWO TO FOUR MONTHS **91**

If you spend a lot of time alone with your baby (either because you are a single parent or because your partner is often away at work), it is important to see whether someone else (a grandparent, uncle, aunt, friend or babysitter) can look in now and then, take your baby for a little while and offer you some time off. If your baby is very young (under three months), it's best if this is always the same person. You can then go out for a walk or shopping, or just take a break and relax. If your baby cries the whole time you are away, it won't hurt, but it's a good idea to let the carer know that he or she should sit down in a comfortable chair, with the baby in his or her arms, and turn on some quiet music.

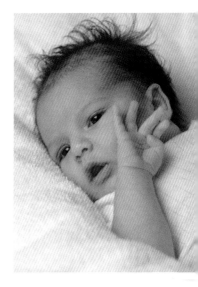

Some parents worry that the mother–child bonding process will be disturbed by teaching a baby to feel separate from his mother. Such worries are unfounded. The development of a strong attachment doesn't depend on mother and baby being alone together as much as possible, but instead involves a baby trusting and feeling secure with the care and companionship of his loved ones.

When your baby is three to four months old, it's good to have finished training him in basic sleeping habits, such as where and when to go to sleep. Normally it's easier to teach a baby these things before three to four months of age than later on.

Around three to four months of age, you will start to notice your baby protesting about certain things more systematically than others. He will start to have an opinion about who puts him to bed and who does various other things for him. He might start showing a fear of men, people with glasses, or people with other special characteristics (see also page 34). It's as if your baby is thinking 'Something is different, and I liked things better the way that they were before. I don't want this.' It's important not to let behaviour like this faze you. It's nothing serious and doesn't merit any particular response.

"A strong attachment between mother and baby does not depend on the mother being the sole carer."

Four-month-old baby girl who is harder and harder to comfort

We have three children – a 17-year-old girl and a 12-year-old boy, and then a baby of four months. She is a very cheerful and happy baby. She has never been ill and has gained weight steadily. Everything connected to sleep has gone well until now. She has always been quite lively and has wanted to be held a lot, either by us or by her brother or sister. She also gets unhappy quickly if she is alone, but she has never had to wait long for attention.

Now in the last weeks this has started to change. She is more difficult about going to bed in the evenings, doesn't want to fall asleep while breastfeeding as she was used to doing, and cries regardless of what we do. We've tried everything, even putting her in the car and driving around, and pushing her in her pram (I don't know what people think when they see her father outside walking her through the neighbourhood at 11 p.m.). It doesn't matter what we do, it always takes about two hours to get her to fall asleep. Sometimes, she might doze for 20 minutes, but then it all starts again. But she sleeps well for the rest of the night, from about midnight, when she finally falls asleep. She still breastfeeds once or twice during the night. Previously she would always fall asleep peacefully while breastfeeding at about 9:30 p.m. We'd put her in her cot and she'd keep on sleeping. She's also become more fretful during the day and harder to comfort. She used to take her naps while I went with her for a walk, but now if the pram ever stops moving she wakes up. We've taken her to the doctor but he couldn't find anything wrong with her.

We hope that you can give us some advice.

ARNA'S ANSWER

I think there are three possible reasons for the change in her behaviour.

The first is the times of the day when she sleeps. The timing of her naps could be out of balance. You don't mention anything about this in the letter, but it's possible that her falling asleep so late in the evening might be disturbing her daytime nap routine.

The second is her temperament. You say that she has a happy and cheerful disposition but also that she is lively and likes to keep busy. Quite often the parents of a spirited baby respond to her energetically. Probably you're having to bounce her around a lot in the evenings. You do need to engage her high spirits and enterprise, but doing so can create stress rather than moving her towards sleep. In the hope of calming her down, you are actually overstimulating her. This may stop her crying but it does not really calm her.

The third is that she hasn't yet learned to comfort herself. Your baby needs to learn to fall asleep on her own both during the day and at night. Otherwise the risk is that she'll have more and more trouble with her naps and that she'll start waking up more often at night. She's definitely having real problems going to sleep in the evenings. You need to create a plan and follow it for one or two weeks, and see whether she is willing to go along. She's clearly not doing well with the current situation.

I'll go over these three issues and how you can work on each of them.

Times of day when she sleeps: There should be a regular pattern to the timing of when she sleeps. She should wake up at a particular time in the morning, such as 8 a.m. (an appropriate time if she was previously falling asleep at 9:30 p.m.). After she wakes up in the morning, she should stay awake for two hours, until 10 a.m. Then she should wake up from her last nap at 6 p.m. (if she takes three naps) and will be ready to turn in for the night around 10 p.m. It's good to start by fixing these four points in the daily routine, that is, when she wakes up, when she takes her first nap, when she wakes up from her last nap and when she goes to bed. Later you can slowly move these timings earlier if you want.

Temperament: She is a lively baby and when there's something that she can't do, she demands even more service from you than she normally gets. You need to train her to relax. You can do this by, for example, always making her wait a little for things – just for a minute or two. If you are washing your hair or Daddy is putting clothes in the washing washine, you should finish what you are doing rather than rushing to help her, even if she is making her wishes known very loudly. Let her be in the same room with you, so that she can watch what you're doing, but don't run to her if she complains about poor service or boredom. On the other hand, you do need to satisfy her need for exercise and activity. It's good to put her on her tummy on a rug or mat and let her fend for herself. You might do this for 10 or 15 minutes two to three times a day. You can stay with her, but don't pick her up. Just stay nearby and show her some toys or something else that's interesting. She wants to be bigger than she is, and in order to do more and more things she needs to practise. It's all right if she gets angry, as with anger comes energy which will probably propel her forwards to learn new things even more quickly.

Learning to comfort herself: You need to slowly reduce the amount that you rock her during her naps. The first nap of the day is usually the easiest time to be tough about this. Lay her down in her regular place and teach her to fall asleep there on her own (reducing any rocking little by little). She needs to get used to sleeping undisturbed and in one particular place. Anything else will stress her and prolong the problem of her not sleeping long enough. Sleeping while being pushed around in a pram is equivalent to falling asleep (and staying asleep) while being rocked. Next, choose a few days or evenings when her father can put her to bed, three to four nights in a row. I recommend that her father take this on because she is lively and probably rather assertive and is breastfeeding. I also suggest that you not begin too early in the list of steps on pages 60–61. I propose starting with step 12. Before laying her down, you need to leave the house. Daddy should follow a definite bedtime routine, which should take about five minutes and include a hug. A good routine might be to close the curtains, turn off the light, cuddle for a moment and sing one song (always the same song). Then Daddy puts her in her cot, sits with her and tends to her every few minutes until she falls asleep. Right now, when she goes to sleep it takes two hours and many tears, so things can only get better. Her father needs to do this job in an organised and somewhat robotic way, so that she works out as quickly as possible that when the whole ceremony is over she is supposed to go to sleep.

Follow-up letter

We wanted to let you know how things have gone. We made sure that she was always awake from 6 p.m. onwards. Her last nap had started to be pretty late in the day, so that might have been the key step. Then her father took over the job of putting her to bed. She surprised us and barely cried at all the first evening. Her father laid her down and sat with her. The next two evenings went the same. She fell asleep within a few minutes. Then, the following evening, she protested for 40 minutes and we thought that all was lost, but Daddy was very firm and did exactly as you described. I had to cover my ears in the living room. The next evening she protested too, but not for as long. Since then everything has gone very well. Her father is still putting her to sleep and sitting with her, two weeks later. We haven't dared to change that. I tried laying her down to sleep on the tenth evening and she cried for a whole hour, so he took over again.

She is also learning to wait a little for attention during the day, but she isn't happy about this. She cries a lot, and loudly, and I admit that I go to her pretty quickly. During the daytime she is doing a really good job of falling asleep. Usually she needs almost no rocking at all, except sometimes for her third nap, which has become very short. The other two naps go really well and most often she sleeps for two hours each time, sometimes even longer on the first nap.

ARNA'S ANSWER

There's one more thing that I'd like to point out. One reason it's important for you (the mother) not to rush too quickly to her when she fusses during the day, but rather to make her wait a little, is that this is connected to her behaviour in the evenings when she is going to sleep, when she wants more service from you than from others. Of course, you should respond to a crying baby, but it's best to do it in an unhurried way. It is enough, for example, to pick her up, or lie down next to her if she is playing on the floor, and show her something or sing to her. It's also good to make a point of going to her and admiring what she is doing when she is busy playing (but without disturbing her concentration). Don't give her too much of a chance to use crying to get what she wants.

If you put her down to sleep, it might be good to have her father on backup duty while you and she get used to working together. If you put her to sleep, and she really protests, then he takes over after 15 or 20 minutes and finishes the job. If she sees the two of you present a united front she will learn what she needs to do.

Four month old who wakes up more and more often at night

We came to you three years ago with our son, who is now four. It wasn't easy to teach him to sleep — we have always had to make sure that he goes to sleep at the right time of day, as his sleep gets all messed up with even the slightest change. And that immediately affects his mood during the day. But we've managed to keep him sleeping well by sticking to a strict routine. If he wakes up at night, he has a really hard time getting back to sleep and he is very irritable the next day.

Four months ago his baby sister was born. She slept perfectly well the first three months and everyone was happy, but in the last few weeks she has been waking up more and more often at night — as many as 10 times. It isn't hard to get her to fall asleep again, usually it's enough to give her a dummy and tuck her back in. She feeds once during the night, and wakes up cheerful and full of energy in the morning but we can't say the same for ourselves. She sleeps well during the day and falls asleep on her own both in the evening and for her naps. We made sure to teach her this right from the beginning and to create a clear sleeping routine. She doesn't seem to be as sensitive about disturbances as her brother was. I had to take her on a trip abroad when she was two months old and she acted as if nothing was different.

Why is she having problems sleeping now? Why is this happening to us again? We seem not to be able to have a child who sleeps and we are also worried that she might start waking up her brother. He sleeps in another room, but he can wake if she cries. What do we keep doing wrong?

ARNA'S ANSWER

It's not unusual for parents who have had one baby who slept very poorly to worry about the same thing happening with their next child. Nobody wants to have to go through this again. It seems that it's really still her big brother's sleep sensitivity which is the issue. When your little girl started to move around more and make more noise during the night, which happens often when babies reach four months of age, you started to respond to her more and more, mainly because you were worried that any commotion from her would wake up her brother with all the problems that would cause. You probably then started to go to her more often and more quickly than necessary. You say she is a very calm baby, or at least it's always easy to get her to fall asleep again, and she isn't sensitive about changes.

Look at how you respond: In order to put a stop to this waking before it becomes a habit, you should take a good look at how you respond to your baby at night, and then do only half of what you normally do. If, for example, you always fix her bedclothes, pat and hush her and give her a dummy when she wakes up at night, start by just giving her the dummy and hushing her. You probably aren't

conscious of how much you are assisting your baby, especially as you're worried that her noise will wake her brother. You want to stop the chain of events as quickly and surely as possible.

Also, don't rush to her too quickly, especially early in the night. Don't tamper with the night-time feed, but do try to keep it from happening too early in the night. Later on you can see whether you can move it steadily towards morning and eventually merge it into her morning feed.

See whether just stepping down the level of service works. Do less and less and wait longer and longer before tending to her. Most probably your baby won't make a lot of noise, but will just toss and turn a little and then fall back to sleep. She can already fall asleep by herself in the evening and she was sleeping very well before, so it shouldn't take long to see results. Ideally, as you begin this new routine, arrange for your son to spend a couple of nights at his grandparents or another relative. This will reduce your workload and your worries.

Don't blame yourselves: You must, above all, recognise that this isn't your fault. The reason why your son sleeps so precariously is that he is just like this by nature. He is sensitive as far as sleep goes, and he was born that way. You didn't do anything wrong when he was a little baby. What can be done, however, is to learn what he can tolerate and to proceed accordingly. Then, little by little, you can get him used to accepting small deviations from his routine, like sleeping at Grandma and Grandpa's (or at another place he likes). It might be good to let him do that regularly, like once or twice a month.

Follow-up letter

Thank you very much for the excellent advice. We wanted to let you know how things went. Grandma and Grandpa took our son for the weekend, and what do you know, our little girl slept better straight away, even though we didn't tend to her so often. But when her brother came home, she started to wake up more often again so it is clear to us her brother's presence has something to do with this. Perhaps anticipating trouble, we've been jumping up out of bed too quickly to tend to her when he's around.

ARNA'S ANSWER

That she slept better with less tending is key to the situation. It is good that you realised that you increased your services when her brother came home (and had been doing so all along). Your arousal threshold is higher when your son is not at home and consequently your daughter has more space to do whatever she does in her sleep (move around or make some sounds) without you responding. I want to suggest one more thing that has worked well for some parents who are in similar circumstances – that is to move your little girl into her own room as soon as possible. At any rate, move her bed as far from yours as you can. The point of doing this is so that she can toss and turn in her sleep as much as she needs or wants, without any interference. Something that can also work well is to play soft music during the night in the hallway between your kids' rooms, basically to reduce the chance that sounds from one child will disturb the other.

Five to eight months

Now that your baby is older and more settled, she will be ready to reduce, and possibly stop altogether, night-time feeds, although she might need a little help from you to do this. At around this age, too, her need for daytime naps reduces from three to two a day.

NIGHT-TIME FEEDS

When your baby is five to six months old, start reducing night-time feeds. Usually a baby who is five to six months old and weighs at least 7–7.5 kilos, or around 16 pounds, can get through the night (by which I mean 10 to 11 hours) without being fed. Some babies stop feeding at night even earlier, which is also totally normal. It works best to let your baby lengthen the time that she needs between feeds. She should reduce, little by little, the number of times she feeds until just one night feed is left. This last feed should take place steadily later and later during the night, until it simply merges with the first morning feed. Some babies do this more or less by themselves but others need a little help from their parents. To help this process along, you should try not to feed your baby too early in the night and use other ways of consoling her before you resort to feeding.

If, on the other hand, your baby starts at this time to make a regular habit of waking up more and more often and demanding to be fed, you need to think about putting a stop to her demands. Bear in mind, however, that even when nigh feeds have stopped, it is normal for a baby to want a single extra night feed every now and then.

DAYTIME NAPS

At around five to six months, babies usually go from three daytime naps down to two. The most important factor in how many naps your baby needs is her ability to stay awake – particularly in the morning after a night's sleep. A baby who can stay awake for 1–1½ hours every morning needs three naps. A baby who can stay awake for 2–2½ hours in the morning can start to nap just twice.

When this happens, you will need to push the naps a little later in the day, and your baby will need to go to sleep a little earlier in the evening. Babies usually need to sleep a little longer at night when they start taking just two daytime naps.

Typical sleep and wake times for a
five-month-old baby who has three
daytime naps

This baby sleeps from 9 p.m. to 7 a.m. only waking at around 5 for a short feed. His last nap is only 30 minutes long (at about 5 p.m. and soon he will stop needing this third nap.

    If you are wondering whether this is also the case for your baby, common signs are: if her third nap has become very short (less than half an hour); if it has become harder to get your baby to fall asleep for her nap; or if your baby is napping later and later in the day so that it starts to affect the time that she goes to sleep in the evening. In all three cases, it is probably time to take another look at the way your baby naps and to take the third, short nap off the schedule. While your baby is getting used to taking two naps, she may still need a third nap now and then, for example on days when her first two naps have been shorter than normal.

"It is just as difficult to calm an overtired baby as
a baby who is not tired enough."

Suppose your baby wakes up at 7 a.m., takes her first nap from 9:30 to 11 a.m., her second nap from 2 to 4 p.m., and goes to sleep for the night at 8 p.m. If, one day, her second nap is very short and she wakes up at 2:30 in the afternoon, she will need a third nap that day. This third nap needs to be as early as possible so as not to disturb her night-time sleep. But if your baby wakes up from her second nap between 3 and 4 p.m., she can stay awake until she goes to sleep for the night. It's not a good idea, however, to let your baby stay awake too long, for example before she goes to sleep in the evening, as she will get too tired. It is just as difficult to calm an overtired baby as a baby who is not tired enough. For a five-month-old baby, staying awake for 3½–4 hours before going to sleep through the night should be about right.

Typical sleep and wake times for a six- to seven-month-old baby who has two daytime naps

This baby has an 1½-hour nap at 9 a.m. and a 2-hour nap at 1 p.m.

Among babies who take two daytime naps, there is a lot of variation in whether both naps are the same length or whether one is longer than the other. It doesn't seem to make any difference how babies divide their sleeping time between their naps. As they get older, most babies shorten one of the two naps, in preparation for giving it up altogether. This shortening of one of the naps usually happens around eight to nine months of age.

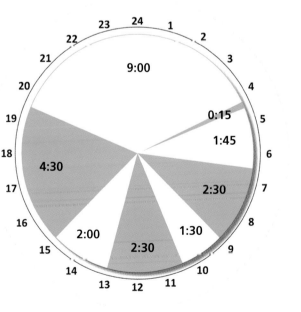

DEVELOPMENTAL FACTORS AFFECTING SLEEP

Changes in the way your baby perceives and explores her environment, as well as the introduction of solids, can affect how well a baby sleeps at this age. Her newly developed willpower may prove testing for you too.

Cognitive development

Around the age of five to six months, babies start to become conscious of their own will and want more say over the way the things around them are organised. Quite commonly at this age, your baby will want the environment she falls asleep in to remain unchanged during the night. If your baby falls asleep while being fed, for example, when she wakes up at night, she'll demand to be fed. She then will start to feed more and more at night, instead of less and less, as would normally be expected of an older baby.

Babies of this age also can have very definite ideas about who should put them to sleep, who should come when they wake up at night and who should care for them in other ways connected to sleep. A baby will always insist on the carer who is with her the most. She does this because she knows, among other things, that only Mummy has milk and so she obviously wants her. At this age, your baby will start to want ever more control over who cares for her and how. Of course, she will just be pushing boundaries here and needs to learn that although she might prefer one parent over the other to do a particular thing for her, that doesn't mean that you will always be able to grant such wishes. You need to calmly stand your ground.

Motor development

Between five and eight months of age, the typical baby learns to sit up and to move around on the floor. Some babies start to crawl during these months and those who are in a real hurry even start to stand in preparation for walking. They also commonly start to move and toss and turn when they are put in their cots to sleep at night. They even start to practise their new abilities half-asleep during the night.

It is important that you don't intervene too quickly when you see your baby moving around in her sleep. She needs to learn by herself how to find the most comfortable way to sleep. You don't want her to learn that when she shifts herself around, someone will come quickly and lay her down again, tuck her in and lull her to sleep (unless you want to keep on providing such service for years to come!). If you need to help your baby lie down and fall back to sleep, it's best to do so with as little fanfare as possible. Do help your baby if her dummy falls out of the cot, but if she kicks her blanket off, just let it be. Don't pull it back up over her. From this age, most babies want to have their blanket underneath them, or beside them, where they can squeeze or knead it with their hands. If you are worried that she will get cold, make sure she sleeps in socks and warm pyjamas.

With her burgeoning new skills, your baby now starts to grope towards an answer to the question of who is in charge in your household. You should treat her attempts at control as signs that she is a quick learner.

Starting solids

Babies of this age change their eating habits dramatically. They first start to eat solid food, then more and more types of it. Most babies get their first taste of solid food around six months (the current recommendation is that babies should be given only milk until the age of six months, but it's important to be flexible to meet your baby's needs). While it is possible to wean a child away from being fed at night before she starts to eat solid food, most parents choose to let these stages overlap. Some babies have a hard time learning to reduce the number of times they feed at night, and don't start to sleep well until all night-time feeding is stopped. Such babies are usually strong-willed and determined. If your baby is like this, stopping night feeds completely may be an easier undertaking than reducing them little by little. However, your baby needs to be at least six months old before all night-time feeding can be cut out so drastically.

For the first days that your baby has solid food, it is best to offer it in the middle of the day so that you can see whether she tolerates that particular type of food. If she gets an upset tummy, it will happen during the day and not at night. For the same reason, when introducing a new food later on, you should do it during the daytime and not the evening. After the first few days of her eating solid food happily, switch over to feeding her in the evening, usually about an hour before putting her to bed for the night. This will both fortify her better for reducing or stopping night feeding and also gives you more reassurance about reducing night feeds.

After about three weeks, add a second solid feed, during the day, usually around noon or in the early afternoon.

When adding a third solid feed, make this in the afternoon if you are breastfeeding and in the morning if you are bottlefeeding. The reason for the difference is that it will help keep up your milk production if your baby gets only breast milk in the mornings. You will have a lot of milk when you wake up and can readily put your baby to your breast for the first two morning feeds.

Nutrition and sleep are closely intertwined for newborn babies. Life is all about sleeping and feeding. As your baby grows, it is good to separate these two spheres of life as much as possible, as otherwise

Typical feeding, sleep and wake times for a seven- to eight-month-old baby

This baby wakes up at 7 a.m. and is breastfed. She has some porridge and is breastfed again before she takes her morning nap. When she wakes up she has milk from a bottle. Around 1 p.m., before she takes her second nap, she has puréed vegetables and/or fruit with a drink of water. After her second nap she has milk from a bottle. She soon gets hungry again and has her supper (puréed vegetables and meat) between 5 and 6 p.m., with water. Before bed she has a bit of porridge, sometimes with banana, and milk from a cup or a bottle.

It is sensible to give a baby milk when she wakes up both from a nap and after her night-time sleep and solids before going to sleep as a child then does not connect falling asleep with drinking from breast or bottle. If she is too tired to drink from a cup or bottle before night-time sleep, it makes sense to change the evening plan a little, by giving her a breast or bottle feed an hour after supper (around 6:30 p.m.). That way the baby will feed more effectively before getting too tired. Then about 30 minutes or one hour later, she should have her nightly porridge (usually just a small portion) and then go to sleep.

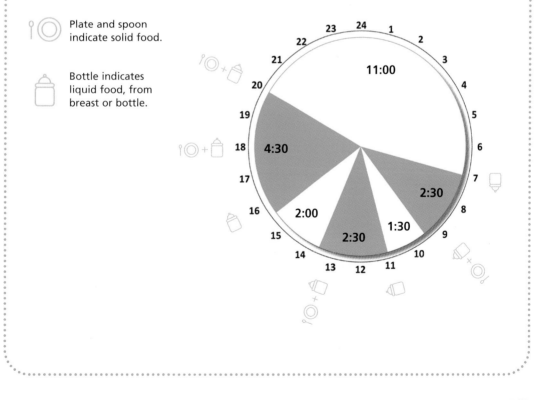

Plate and spoon indicate solid food.

Bottle indicates liquid food, from breast or bottle.

they can interfere with each other; night-time feeding is considered the strongest factor in continued night waking. As your baby gets older and eats solids more frequently, you need to move liquid feeds (bottle or breast) further away from her sleeping hours so that she stops connecting being fed with falling asleep. So that you get the picture, imagine your seven- to eight-month-old baby getting four meals a day. She would be fed solid food before her daytime naps and water or milk from a cup with her food, but breast milk or formula when she wakes up from her naps. She would be fed dinner about two hours after her last nap and a snack 30 to 60 minutes before going to sleep in the evening, to help her get through the night.

Morning feeds can be confusing for babies. If you have recently stopped feeding your baby at night, it is important that you feed her outside her bedroom in the morning. If you feed your baby in her bedroom in the morning and she drops off to sleep afterwards, she might think of it as a night-time feed. The result is that your baby receives a very unclear message – 'Am I allowed to feed at night or not?', she will wonder. And if your child is very strong-willed, she might then think 'If I can feed once, then why not twice, for example, earlier in the night?' A baby who is at least five to six months old and weighs at least 7–7.5 kilos (about 16 pounds) can normally stop night-time feeds. Many babies stop on their own when they are both younger and lighter, and tolerate this very well.

Six month old who takes short and irregular daytime naps

My problem isn't serious but I still wanted to ask whether you could offer some help. The thing is that my six-month-old daughter's daytime naps are very confusing to deal with. We can never count on her sleeping at any particular times. She sleeps well at night, from about 9 p.m. and gets up with us when we wake, which is usually around 8 a.m. but often varies. During the day she just sleeps a little bit here and there, nothing regular. I try to get her to nap once during the day, after noon, but she only sleeps about half an hour. She falls asleep best in the car. She is our first child and I am alone with her during the daytime, and when we go out for a walk or drive to Grandma and Grandpa's or somewhere else, she falls asleep in her buggy or in the car. She always wakes up as soon as we stop walking or the car stops. I've gone back to college in the evenings and it would be great if she could learn to sleep at particular times, so that I could maybe study a little. I'm not hoping for this just for my sake though, as she gets very cranky during the day when she gets virtually no sleep. Is there something I can do to help her sleep better during the day?

ARNA'S ANSWER

Yes, here are a few suggestions, which might help. First of all, you should avoid very irregular waking times in the morning. If necessary, use an alarm to wake up at the same time each day. Then you should decide on one place where she will take her naps (for example, in her pram or cot). Then you should use the sleep and wake cycle illustrations on pages 101 and 102 to work out her nap times. If she wakes up at 8 a.m., you should put her down for her nap at 10 or 10:30. Then put her down again in the same place (the pram or cot) at regular intervals, that is, when she has been awake for 2–2½ hours. Probably she needs three naps to start with and should wake up from her last nap around 5 p.m. and then stay awake for four hours before going to sleep for the night. The goal is to create a steady routine for when she wakes up, when she takes her first nap and when her last nap ends (you already have a regular routine for when she goes to sleep at night, which you shouldn't tamper with).

While you are trying to bring order to her sleeping schedule, it's best to restrict travel around town with her as much as possible, especially early in the day and in the hour or two after she wakes up from a nap (when she will be getting tired again and might fall asleep in the car). Make sure she has her first nap at home.

As for walks and rides in the car, I recommend stopping them while she's napping and instead I suggest taking her out when she has just woken up from a nap so that she can sit up and look out at the world. When you put her to bed during the day, try to keep rocking to a minimum as I discuss on page 66.

Seven month old who wakes up more and more often

When my daughter was around four months she woke up once a night to breastfeed, then went straight back to sleep. Then she started to wake up more often – now, at seven months, it's up to four or five times a night and she feeds most of these times. She always falls asleep on the breast.

She doesn't sleep much during the day – usually three or four 20–30 minute naps. She wakes around 7 a.m. Recently, we've tried to steer her into taking one good nap around noon, then she often has a short nap in the late afternoon. She is happy and cheerful and easy to handle but she is really determined now that only Mummy can put her to sleep (when she was younger, it didn't matter). From around four months, that changed. Now, Daddy can do anything else but not put her to sleep, that's Mummy's job. A few evenings ago we started to put her to sleep around 9 p.m. when she is more awake and that's gone well. Her father stays with her in the bedroom and I sleep in the living room. Now she doesn't wake up as much during the first part of the night. She used to wake up once every hour or two, but since her father took over it is two to three times a night and she doesn't cry as much. During the first part of the night, she gets back to sleep easily after her father gives her a dummy. But after 4 a.m. things get difficult and we let her breastfeed. She usually wakes up again around 6 a.m. and has another feed. Then she wakes up for good around 7 a.m.

For her daytime naps, I take her out for a walk. How should we move ahead now? We haven't yet tried to put her to bed wide awake, for example. Can we teach her to stop waking up at night or is she too young?

ARNA'S ANSWER

You have already started teaching her to fall asleep on her own and also to reduce her night-time breastfeeding, so now you just need to keep at it.

A gentle approach: Yours is a soft approach, which is clearly working well. You should keep putting her in bed when she is more and more awake. Be careful not to let her fall asleep in your arms; if she does, and then wakes up as you put her into bed, she could rouse herself completely and then stay awake until midnight.

She needs to be as ready as possible to go to sleep in the evenings, so you should look at the timing of her naps. Keep on doing things as you are, but choose two times for her naps (see page 102). Her earlier nap is probably too late in the day; don't keep her awake until noon.

Try this for a week or two and see whether things improve in the evenings and at night, just with changing her nap times during the day. Persevere with this if things improve and she wakes up less and less, but if the situation gets worse again, it is probably best to stop breastfeeding at night completely. It would also help her if you stop feeding her in the bedroom, both in the evenings and mornings.

You need to set aside a few days to make all these changes and when you lay her down sleep for the night, awake enough so that she protests, you have to be prepared to hold out. Then sit with her, touching her, but not picking her up. Stay close, hush her, and pat her softly and gently on the back (see also page 63).

Fresh air and naps: As for walks during daytime naps, the danger is that your baby will get used to being rocked to sleep to take a nap. Obviously, you both need fresh air, but it's better to go for a walk when your baby has just woken up so she can sit up, look around and enjoy the sights. In short, it's best if she sleeps in her pram while it's stationary and then goes for a walk when she is awake and not trying to fall asleep. If she has become really used to being rocked and can't fall asleep any other way, you can break this habit little by little (see also page 66).

Follow-up letter

I wanted to let you know how things are going. My daughter's naps have improved a lot: she doesn't need to be rocked to sleep for the first nap and only a little for the second nap. Both naps have become longer, too. She sleeps for two hours before noon and a little over an hour in the afternoon. Falling asleep for the night has also become easier. Now we lay her down and sit with her (it takes longer if just I sit with her; then she tosses and turns and cries more). I find it really hard to listen to her and I worry that she thinks I'm being mean to her, but in the mornings she is always happy and cheerful. She now feeds only at 4 and 6 a.m., and sleeps well all the way up to 4 a.m., which is just great. But we would like to try to move towards having her stop feeding altogether at night. Can you give us any advice on that?

ARNA'S ANSWER

Like most babies, and particularly breastfed ones, your baby makes more demands of her mother. That isn't because you're doing anything wrong, or aren't nice enough to her, you just have something that she wants, and so she tries harder with you. Don't start doing anything new now, like patting her more or talking to her, but keep doing just the same things that her father does. That keeps it simple for her.

With night-time feeding, you might want to decide that on particular nights, say at weekends, her father will take her when she wakes up at 4 a.m., so that you can try to move her 4 a.m. feed to 5 a.m. This is a way of gradually merging the two feeds. Most likely it won't be hard for you to slowly and steadily reduce these feeds given how well everything has gone so far.

Eight month old allowed only one nap at nursery

I'm having difficulties with my eight-month-old daughter. She has always been very easy as far as sleep is concerned and in general no problem to handle. She started nursery a month ago and all the babies are supposed to sleep from 11 a.m. to 2 p.m. She was used to getting up at 7 a.m., sleeping for an hour starting around 9:30 a.m., and then napping again from 2 to 4 p.m. She went to sleep for the night at 8 p.m. She likes nursery very much and does sleep for three hours as they wish, but when we pick her up at 4 p.m. she is very tired and clearly needs to go to sleep again. At first we tried to keep her awake, but it is really hard and usually impossible. We've let her fall asleep around 5 or 6 p.m., and then she goes to sleep for the night at 8 or 8:30. This would be fine if she weren't now waking up at night, usually around 2 a.m., and then sometimes staying awake for a couple of hours. She cries and often seems not to know what she wants. Naturally she's exhausted when she has to get up in the morning and we've started letting her sleep a little longer, which means that one of us gets to work late.

What can we do here? We used to sleep well but now everything is in total chaos. We are happy with the nursery: the manager told us when we applied that all her kids had to take a nap at 11 a.m., and we thought that would work fine. Our daughter is the youngest baby there. All the others are at least a year old. We took her to the doctor, because we thought she might be unwell, but they couldn't find anything wrong.

ARNA'S ANSWER

The best thing would be if you could get the nursery to agree to let your baby nap twice a day for a month or two, until she can start taking just one nap a day without difficulty. It's often possible to keep easy babies like yours awake, as in your case from 7 to 11 a.m., but if a baby is not old enough, it can disturb her sleep at other times, as you have found. One nap a day is almost never enough for babies under about ten months. Some can tolerate it with difficulty, if there are no other complicating factors (including minor disturbances like a cold), but it is always difficult for babies to be forced into a routine for which they aren't developmentally ready.

It is very good that you were told about the nursery's routine in advance, and hopefully you will manage to agree with the carers about making a temporary exception for your little girl. If not, you could try to have her sleep at night from 9 p.m. to 8 a.m., take a nap from 11 a.m. to 1 p.m. (waking her up at 1 p.m.), and having her take another nap from 4 to 5 p.m. Try this routine; these timings should work for a baby of this age. In a month or so, you can shorten the second nap to 30 minutes (from 4 to 4.30). A few weeks later she can start taking just one nap and this should fit in with the other children at the nursery.

Eight-month-old baby who still feeds during the night

I have an eight-month-old daughter who is a calm and easy baby. She is healthy and a good sleeper. She goes to bed at 8 p.m. and falls asleep on her own in her bed. She wakes up once a night, usually around 5 a.m. I feed her and she falls straight back to sleep. This is no problem for me. Sometimes she doesn't wake up until around 6 a.m. Afterwards, she sleeps on until around 8 a.m. Then we get up and I give her breakfast.

Recently when I took her for a check-up, the staff advised me to stop feeding her at 5 a.m.

because she is old enough to manage without it. I thought they were making too much of a big deal about this but my friends who have babies of the same age, have also been telling me that I should stop feeding my daughter at night. They say it would only take three nights, and that the best way is to let her father sleep with her for the night while I sleep out in the living room. They also say they got this advice from you. Is it really necessary that all babies who are at least six months old and weigh 7.5 kilos, or 16 pounds, should stop feeding at night?

ARNA'S ANSWER

It's like getting your driving licence; you can take the test when you reach the minimum age, but you don't have to. Seriously, it's not necessary to stop feeding an eight-month-old baby at night. You need to look at the whole picture for each individual baby. As babies get older, drinking milk from a bottle at night isn't good for their teeth and can start to disturb their sleep, too. They wake up wanting something to drink, and don't always have an easy time falling asleep again. Your little girl is both young enough and calm enough that I wouldn't worry about these things for now.

It's also clear that she's slowly moving the 5 a.m. feed later and later in the night. If you are relaxed, too, you probably aren't rushing to her at 5 a.m., but instead taking a little time before you respond to her. Just go with it if little by little she drinks less and/or pushes the feed later – this whole issue is not a big deal for you two. If you want to gently encourage her to stop feeding, let her wait a little when she wakes up at 5 a.m. Perhaps she'll fall asleep again. You can also always offer her a dummy first and see whether that's enough to help her fall back to sleep.

If she uses a bottle, you can also fill it less and less full (for example, by 10 ml a week) or progressively thin out the milk with water until she is getting just water. Then you can start reducing the amount of water if she doesn't lose interest on her own. If your baby is breastfed, you can offer water in a cup.

Rules about what a baby should do or be able to do at a given age are actually just benchmarks or averages. Parents have to work out what is most appropriate for them and their baby. Most people like to give advice and we particularly like to give advice about what has gone well for ourselves. Most of us also like to keep things simple. You see this reflected in the idea that every baby should be able to do a given thing at a given age. But you are all doing fine; you both sleep well and the morning feed isn't an issue for you. So I recommend that you keep up what you are doing.

Eight month old who 'grazes' all night

Our little 'prince' is eight months old. He is a very busy, energetic boy, who's always on the go. He's happiest when there are a lot of people around him and a lot going on. He has always fed every three to four hours at night though we have tried to cut this down lately by making the first night feed a little later. This hasn't worked at all – he just turns up the volume. He doesn't want his father anywhere near him during the night. I breastfeed him, and he knows that only Mummy has milk.

He's sleeping in our bed, I go to sleep at the same time as he does, and he breastfeeds whenever he wants, which is quite often. It would be more or less OK if he fell asleep in between feeds, but instead he's always on the move. He can stand now and I'm afraid that he'll fall out of the bed (this actually happened once but fortunately he didn't hurt himself). He's taken over almost the whole bed; I sleep on the edge with one eye open to make sure that he doesn't fall out while his father sleeps in the living room. This isn't a good situation, and it's started affecting us all. Our son is cranky and his father and I are irritable with each other and perennially tired. Now my parents are going abroad and we're house-sitting for three weeks. We thought this might be a good time to try improving the sleep situation. Can you give us some advice?

P.S. During the day, he falls asleep on his own and regularly sleeps well for an hour in the morning, and a couple of hours in the afternoon.

ARNA'S ANSWER

It doesn't always work to use gentle methods to reduce the number of night feeds. When dealing with very active and headstrong babies, gentleness often fails. It's a good idea, however, to use the opportunity of house-sitting to make a change. When dealing with a determined baby, you have to be very determined yourself and give simple, clear, messages. Follow the 10-point plan opposite, which I hope will help improve things.

In this plan, your son's father will be doing most of the 'work' but there are a couple of things that are important for you. First, don't let your son see you until you breastfeed him in the morning (outside the bedroom). Then, after his morning feed, he needs to stay awake for 2½ hours before taking a nap.

And, above all, make sure you give him a lot of attention during the day, and be generous with hugs and kisses.

Note: There are even tougher approaches than this one (see page 56), in which the father leaves the room after the baby is put to bed and then comes in at predetermined intervals.

As far as a baby is concerned, whether his carer stays in the room or leaves makes a considerable difference, and most often it works better if the father stays. That's the more gentle

10-point plan to better sleep habits

This is a considerably stricter approach than has been recommended in other letters:

1 Go to the doctor for a check-up to rule out any illness. You don't want to start acting strict and then find out that your baby is poorly.

2 Don't change anything with his naps. Regardless of how the nights go, keep his nap times the same.

3 He needs to go outside to play once a day after one of his naps. For example, go to a playground where his father can swing on the swings with him in his arms, or something else that he'll enjoy: keeping his days busy will increase the likelihood that the nights will be peaceful.

4 Decide where he should fall asleep, for example, in a particular room, in his cot, with his father sleeping in the same room.

5 In the evening he should have dinner about 6 p.m. He can breastfeed after that, say at 7 p.m. I would not breastfeed him just before sleep but you could give him a snack – I'd recommend warm oatmeal (see page 41) – at 8 p.m. (about half an hour before going to sleep).

6 You say good night to him and Daddy, and leave the house at 7:30 p.m. (Even if Daddy is supposed to put him to sleep, it won't work if he knows that you are in the next room.) He's at the ideal point for going to sleep when he has been awake for about 4½ hours (from 4 to 8:30 p.m.).

7 Daddy takes him into the bedroom and does all the usual things (closes the curtains, turns off the light, sings a song and hugs him) then puts him into bed and goes to sit on a chair by the door. Your son will get upset and/or angry, but Daddy stays sitting there, whatever happens.

8 About every four minutes he stands up and gently lays your son back down, gives him his dummy (if he uses one) and stays in physical contact with him for half a minute. Then he sits down again and waits another four minutes.

9 Daddy repeats this until your son falls asleep, however long it takes.

10 Daddy sleeps in the room with your son. When your son wakes up in the night, Daddy does the same things that he did when he put him in bed in the evening. He waits, lays your son back down and gives him his dummy. He repeats this for as long as it takes for your son to fall asleep.

approach and more acceptable for all concerned. Still, it doesn't work in all cases.

Some babies get more upset and angry if a parent just sits there and does nothing, as if thinking 'Why on earth are you sitting there if you aren't going to do anything for me?' A baby like this will cry more if the parent is sitting in the room than if the parent leaves. In these cases it's obviously better to leave the room than to provoke more crying by sitting with the baby.

Follow-up letter

Thanks for your very precise advice. We're a week into the new approach now. There were very loud protests the first evening our son was alone with his father and he didn't want to back down, but his father put in his headphones to listen to music, and sat calmly. On the second evening there was some improvement. Since then he has made progress every evening, until last night, when he screamed again for half an hour but then slept through the whole night. The nights have varied. Mostly he has woken up some time after 4 a.m., but I haven't fed him and now he is more interested in having his father lay him down again and give him his dummy. Then he falls asleep again. We are wondering whether his father is going to be stuck with having to do this forever. We can totally imagine our little prince demanding something like that!

ARNA'S ANSWER
So that his father doesn't get stuck in this role, Dad should reduce what he does, for example, he should put the dummy in your son's hand but not in his mouth. He should also start lengthening slightly the time that he waits. In short, he should respond more slowly and do less. Dad can also start to train your son to accept him going out of sight while he's falling asleep (see pages 46–47). Also make sure, when you get back to your own home again, you change the location of your son's cot. This will help him to avoid falling back into his old habits again. (See also pages 68–69 about changing bad habits.)

Nine to 14 months

At this age, a healthy baby should be able to get through the night without feeding. If your baby is still feeding at night, his waking up during the night to feed just as he has done since he was very little, is simply a habit (see also breaking habits on pages 68–69). It's easiest to discontinue – rather than try to reduce – night feeds and also stop feeding your baby in bed in the mornings, or more accurately, you should move this feed out of the bedroom. Not feeding at all in the bedroom – no bottles or breastfeeding day or night – sends your baby the clearest possible message.

CHANGES TO SLEEP PATTERNS

Parents often wonder how long a baby normally sleeps at night. The length of night-time sleep usually stays relatively stable from about six months of age to three or four years – approximately 11 hours, give or take about an hour. By the time a baby is nine months old, he usually has stopped feeding at night. The changes in sleep patterns from nine to 14 months of age all involve daytime sleep: there is less of it, and babies stop needing two naps and start getting by on one. This change is usually complete around a child's first birthday.

There are two indicators that signal when your baby is ready for these changes: he starts to battle against sleep at his second nap, and he wants to go to bed later in the evening. To get by on one nap, your baby needs to be able to stay awake for four hours after he wakes up in the morning and for six to seven hours before going to bed for the night. When your baby starts taking just one nap, his night-time sleep will usually lengthen by 30 to 60 minutes; often you will notice that his night-time sleep shortens a little in the weeks before this happens.

"At this age, it is usually not enough to reduce night feeds; you must discontinue them altogether."

Typical sleep and wake times for a 10-month-old baby who is almost ready for only one daytime nap

It's typical for a baby who is about ready to move down to just one daytime nap to start sleeping up to an hour less at night. The baby in the top diagram falls asleep at 9 p.m. and wakes up at 7 a.m. Then he takes a 1½-hour nap from 10 to 11:30 a.m. and later another short ½-hour nap from 3:30 to 4 p.m. He isn't particularly tired at 10 a.m., so getting him to fall asleep for his second nap has become something of a battle.

The baby in the bottom diagram wakes up at 7 a.m., takes a short nap at 10 a.m. and then a 2-hour nap from 1:30 to 3:30 p.m. He is not always interested in taking a nap at 10 a.m. and it also has become harder for him to fall asleep for the night.

If your baby is like this, it's worth trying to get him to take just one nap. It's good to use a weekend day (if your baby attends a nursery and you are home at the weekend) to try this out. The nap should start 4 hours after he wakes up, that is, at about 11 a.m. Then he should go to sleep for the night a little earlier, at around 8 p.m.

When babies shift from two naps to one, it's normal for there to be a few weeks where they take one nap on some days and two naps on others. In such cases, there are a couple of rules of thumb.

First, if your baby wakes up from a nap before 1 p.m., he will need to take another nap (in other words, he will not be able to stay awake until bedtime). Second, if your baby cannot stay awake for 3½ hours in the morning before his nap, then he will need to take two naps that day.

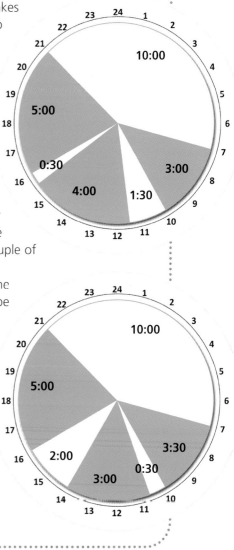

DEVELOPMENTAL FACTORS AFFECTING SLEEP

At nine to 14 months, both separation anxiety and mobility skills – in particular, the ability to stand and possibly walk – may have an effect on your baby's sleep patterns.

Separation anxiety

A baby who starts to feel anxious or afraid when he is left alone is said to be suffering from separation anxiety. The reason he feels this is that he does not yet understand that things that disappear (parents or others) from sight continue to exist. A baby of this age is learning that things continue to exist although they disappear from sight and this knowledge may disturb some babies' sleep (see page 34). This is particularly true if your baby is cautious by nature and adjusts relatively slowly to new things. If this is the case, your baby will start to protest when left alone to sleep and then either you or your partner will need to be in sight while your baby falls asleep. Bear in mind, however, that your baby needs someone nearby, but no more than that. He doesn't need to be rocked, given something to drink or any other extra service, although he probably won't refuse if you offer any of these things. So it's best to avoid offering him anything, as otherwise you risk his reluctance to let go of the service even after he gets over the separation anxiety.

Separation anxiety can also start to disturb a baby's night-time sleep, although this is rarer. In such cases, your baby will start to cry in his sleep as if he is scared. We don't know why a baby starts to do this, but a likely explanation is that he is dreaming about what he experienced during the day or other things that are on his mind. You need to be sure not to do too much for your baby when this happens. You shouldn't, for example, talk to him in a questioning way (as it will seem like you want an answer) or pick him up. It's enough just to hush him and lay your hand on him affectionately. What your baby needs is a feeling of security. He doesn't need something to drink, or to be carried around the house. Always start by waiting for a moment to see whether your baby stops crying on his own. Often it's enough to just stay in bed (if he sleeps in your room) or to go to his doorway (if he's in his own room) and say 'Shhh, everything's OK, Mummy is here.' Frequently it will be enough if your baby hears your voice; he is aware of yours and your partner's voices in sleep and will be calmed by them. If, however, you go in and tend to your baby, touching him can wake him up completely.

It takes a varying amount of time for separation anxiety to pass: depending on the individual, it may take up to several months. Bear in mind that the most successful approach is to give your baby just what he needs at night, and no more.

Learning to stand

Sleep patterns may be disturbed when your baby learns to stand up as he may start to use this new ability at inappropriate times. When he is put to bed for the night, he may stand up straight away and expect lots of praise for doing so, just as he does when showing off a new skill or ability during the day. But you will not be as thrilled at this time. Often, your baby will stand up over and over again and you will lay him back down until one of you – usually the parent – gets tired of the whole thing. Sometimes it will work to hold your baby down for a moment to get him to fall asleep. More commonly, you will walk out, leaving him standing there alone and protesting, or (even more commonly) you will pick him up and take him out of the room.

The same thing can happen during the middle of the night, too. Half-asleep, your baby will stand up and you will respond quickly by rushing to lay him down again before he wakes up completely, in the knowledge that it could take ages to get him to fall asleep again if he becomes wide awake. As soon as you start to respond to your baby so quickly, you run the risk that he will make a habit of always standing up when he half-wakes at night, because he has started to expect that you will then come and settle him down again.

If you lay your baby down and he stands up again, it's best to ignore this as long as possible, and act as if you haven't noticed. Let him stand (or sit, or toss and turn) and just leave him alone. If he doesn't start crying, then don't go to him. If he does start crying, wait for at least a few minutes and then go to him, pat his mattress and say 'Lie down'. He will look at you and won't understand what has got into you, but only the first time. Say 'Lie down' again and help him to lie down, but don't help him too much. Don't say anything else and don't look him in the eye. Once he is lying down, give him his dummy or anything else that he uses as a comfort object, and then wait quietly somewhere else in the room. If he stands up again, act again as if nothing is happening for a few minutes; then repeat the 'Lie down' routine. The longer this takes, the longer you should wait before going to assist him. Don't scold, and keep your tone and expression as neutral as possible. You can respond in the same way if your baby stands up during the middle of the night.

Babies learn to stand up before learning to sit down again, so often need assistance. It can take some weeks until your baby can easily sit down by himself. So if you need to help your child to sit down, do this as he will when he has learned the skill. Don't take your baby in your arms and lay him down then put his blanket over him. Just help your baby to sit down with as little fuss as possible and let him roll to a lying position. If you want to help your baby perfect the skill of sitting down, do so in the daytime.

10 month old still having several night feeds

Our son is 10 months old and still wakes up to breastfeed at night, sometimes as much as every half hour during the later parts of the night. He doesn't really need anything to drink but I am so exhausted and he cries so loudly, that I do it to get him to stop crying. It would be OK if he would just fall asleep, but he stays awake on my breast, more or less, from 4 a.m. onwards. We've been told over and over that we shouldn't pick him up and take him out of his cot when he wakes up, and that after three nights of not doing this he would stop demanding my breast. We just don't believe this. He is such a relaxed and gentle baby that we don't want to use such a tough approach.

A week ago we decided to start working on a better sleep routine. Fixing the timing of his naps went well (they were not regular) and so did teaching him to fall asleep on his own during the day. He is happy with being put down for his nap and falls asleep straight away. Falling asleep in the evenings without us also works well, but the early morning problems haven't gone away. Just denying him feeding till around 4 a.m. hasn't worked, and now he is in our bed from 4 a.m. onwards. Can you think of anything else that we could try? He seems to need so much closeness and snuggling. We don't want to deny him that.

ARNA'S ANSWER

As you yourselves realise, breastfeeding plays a big role in your current problems.

Your baby is now too old to learn to breastfeed just once during the night, so you will have to discontinue all night feeds (see the three-point plan opposite). It is easier for a baby to learn to stop breastfeeding completely at night than to learn to feed just once or twice. I would advise you to leave the house while your baby's Daddy puts him to bed in the evening; that way, he won't sense that you are around and will be less likely to call for you during the night. It's best if it's clear to your son from the evening routine who will be caring for him during the night. He has already learned to fall asleep on

Three-point plan to discontinuing night breastfeeding

There are three essentials in stopping night feeds:

1 Completely uncouple breastfeeding and sleep – only offer your baby the breast when he is wide awake and not in a mood to fall asleep.

2 Completely stop breastfeeding while lying down.

3 Move all breastfeeding out of the bedroom.

his own, and probably won't have any trouble doing so without you.

Concentrate solely on discontinuing breastfeeding at night, and keep everything else the same. This means that Daddy can pick up your boy and give him all the closeness and cuddling that he needs. He just won't get to breastfeed. Daddy can offer him water in a cup (not a bottle), although he probably won't want any. In short, Daddy can do everything with your son except take him out of the bedroom or get Mummy.

Keep in mind that you're not giving your son to a stranger, but to his father, and getting through the night together, without breast milk, will strengthen the attachment between the two of them. It's best if you can stay somewhere else for two or three nights while this adjustment is taking place.

Follow-up letter

It's amazing. Father and son are sleeping together in our bed and sleeping well. He protested twice, for an hour each time, during the first night but his father says that it wasn't actually as much or as loud as he had expected. He cried more if he was offered water, so his father stopped trying that. Now we're six nights along. I slept at my sister's for three nights and the last three nights I've been in the living room. I don't dare disturb them. Our little fellow has woken up cheerful and happy in the morning – a little earlier than usual, but that's not a big problem. He has a breastfeed, not in the bedroom and not lying down, then some porridge, and he is very happy with the whole arrangement. We are wondering whether we should let him sleep with us or put him in his own bed. I think it would be better to put him in his own bed so that we don't fall back into the old pattern again.

Thanks very much for your help.

One year old wakes up at night and can't get back to sleep for hours

My daughter is a little over a year old, and she has just started to wake up at night and stay awake for a long time. She usually wakes up around 2 a.m. and stays awake for one, two or even three hours. Generally she isn't restless or unhappy; she just doesn't want to sleep. She wants to get out of bed and play.

This is a girl who falls asleep on her own in the evenings. Her sleeping times are like this: she falls asleep around 8 p.m. then wakes up around 2 and stays awake until 4 a.m. If she stays awake for a long time at night, which she usually does, then we have to wake her up to go to nursery at 7:30 a.m. Then she sleeps there from 10 a.m. to noon. Back at home she takes a nap from about 3 to 5 p.m. although it varies in length. Still she is always ready to go to bed at 8 p.m. What do you think could be the reason? She is happy at nursery and has no problems sleeping there. She is a very cheerful and obedient girl. The nursery staff are willing to help us if there is something they can do to improve things.

At the weekend she sleeps longer in the mornings, often until 10 a.m., and then she just has one nap, typically from 1 to 4 p.m., but she doesn't sleep any better at night at the weekend.

ARNA'S ANSWER

Your letter doesn't tell me what triggered her night-time waking, but I can see what is keeping it going. Her sleep timings are not quite right and vary between weekdays and weekends. This may not have been the issue to begin with, but it is what's causing her to keep waking up for such a long time at night.

Shorten her second nap to an hour straight away, and after a few days cut it down to half an hour. If it becomes hard to wake her up after such a short time, just shorten the nap time more slowly, say in 10-minute increments. Usually it is best to wake up a sleeping baby by turning on the light, taking her in your arms and talking calmly for a while, then getting more and more active.

Wake her always at the same time in the morning, every day of the week. If the length of her night is more than 12 hours (you say that sometimes at the weekend she goes to bed at 8 p.m. and wakes up at 10 a.m., which is 14 hours), that's enough to enable her to spend two to three of these hours awake. Aim for her to be able to take just one daytime nap within a week or two. This should be roughly from 11 a.m. to 2 p.m. Be sure, too, to avoid responding to her too energetically at night. Do as little as you can.

One year old has difficulty falling asleep after an ear infection

Our boy slept well until two months ago, when he was ten months old, and got an ear infection. He's had difficulty falling asleep since then. Recently, after we lay him down to sleep, he has been standing straight back up. We have had to go so far as to sit next to him and hold him down so that he doesn't stand up immediately. If we do that he falls asleep quickly. I have a feeling that he's anxious in some way. He cries painfully if we leave the room while he's falling asleep, which we try sometimes. Before the ear infection we just laid him down to sleep in his bed. We could leave the room, he would fall asleep on his own, and he slept all night. I don't want to take a tough approach and let him cry, as we've been advised to do. Can you offer some advice?

P.S. We took him to an ear, nose and throat doctor yesterday who said that his ears looked fine.

ARNA'S ANSWER

There may be a combination of factors causing the problem here. It could be the ear infection, and also the fact that he has learned to stand up. It could also be separation anxiety (see page 117. You can check whether separation anxiety is involved by using the method on page 34. That will make you more secure about how to respond to the problem.

It's probably best to sit with him and not try to leave the room while he falls asleep, at least for a few weeks. You'll see then whether he gets calmer and more reassured about going to sleep. I'd also advise that you stop holding him down until he falls asleep. After you have put him down, then you should sit down and, after he stands up, wait for a few minutes. Then you can stand up, lay him down, and give him his dummy or comfort object. Repeat this until he falls asleep.

Usually it's best if the parent who less often puts a baby to bed takes on this role for the first few evenings. The other parent should leave the house before the baby is put to bed, in order to rule out any possibility of assistance that the baby thinks he might be able to demand. Whoever puts your son to bed shouldn't look him in the eye or talk to him, but instead just sit with him and perhaps hush him or hum a tune. It's good if he senses that one of you is there and that you are peaceful and calm.

"At this age, some babies need the reassurance of a parent's presence to fall asleep, for a few weeks."

15 to 24 months

During the second year of life babies normally sleep for 11–11½ hours at night, give or take an hour. The length of their night-time sleep generally stays constant during this period but they slowly and gradually start to sleep less during the day. The vast majority of children continue to take a daytime nap beyond their second birthday, but the occasional child stops earlier, perhaps as young as 18 months. Nap length varies from baby to baby, but can be up to three hours a day. Parents of babies who sleep poorly at night sometimes try to discontinue daytime naps in the hope that their baby will sleep better at night, but this rarely works. If a baby is made to stop napping during the day before she is sufficiently mature, she may start to nod off for a few moments late in the day. This often happens in the car or when they are alone in quiet surroundings. You may not notice these little snoozes but there is a risk that they almost always lower the quality of a baby's night-time sleep. A baby will either start to wake up during the night or start to have a hard time falling asleep in the evening.

For babies at this age, you need to make sure that the longest period your baby spends awake is the one before she settles down for the night. These babies have just one nap, so they are awake for just two stretches during the day; the later stretch (before going to bed for the night) should be longer than the earlier one (before nap time).

DEVELOPMENTAL FACTORS AFFECTING SLEEP

Mastering motor skills such as walking, and possibly climbing, as well as your baby's growing sense of independence, can have an impact on her sleep in a number of ways.

Motor development

A baby at this age finds it easier and easier to move around. Your baby will normally have started to walk and climb, and she will be more secure in her movements. This can affect her sleep. She'll test out her new skills and abilities both while awake and asleep. She may move around a lot during sleep and may even bump into the bars of her cot, quite noisily; she may be neither completely awake nor asleep when this happens. Whenever you need to tend to your baby in this half-asleep state, take care not to wake her up completely. It's best to approach her silently and to make as little contact with her as possible while rearranging her in bed. Ideally, you want to make her feel as if she has lain back down on her own to go back to sleep.

Typical sleep and wake times for an 18-month-old baby

This baby wakes up at 8 a.m., stays awake for 4 hours, and then has a nap from noon to 2 p.m. Then she stays awake for 6½ hours before going to sleep for the night (most babies this age spend six to seven hours awake in the afternoon). She goes to bed about 8:30 p.m.

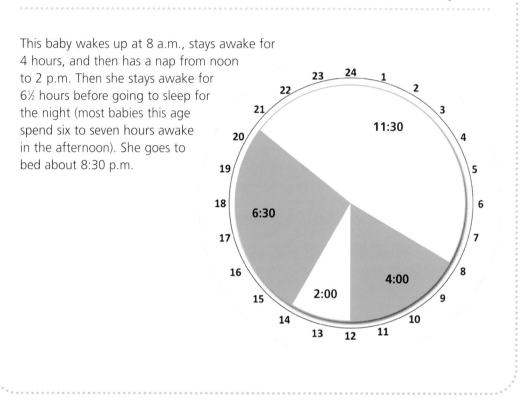

Move her down gently, don't tuck her in and don't pull up her covers if she has kicked them off but put her blanket by her side. It's good if her dummy falls into her hands as if by magic; then she'll put it in her mouth herself if she wants.

Cognitive development

Your baby will begin to have stronger and stronger opinions about how she wants things to be. You shouldn't discourage this battle for independence nor try to break your baby's will; it's better if she develops a strong and secure sense of self. At the same time, however, your baby has to realise that she isn't in charge of everything and that the world doesn't entirely revolve around her. You need to keep in mind that she needs to have the security that comes from parents who lay down rules and guidelines in the home and give clear and simple messages, act consistently, and at the same time have realistic expectations of their children.

A baby will usually start to feel out her position in the household and see whether the limits that have been set are really followed, or whether it's possible to cause them to be changed. Some babies are constantly checking to see how far they can get; others don't. It's very common for your baby to test your limits when she is supposed to go to bed for the night; for example, she'll send you on various errands or ask you to do various things. She may want to be read not just one story but several more, or ask that her back be stroked, and then her forehead, and then her foot just a little, or she may call out for her other parent, who is now also supposed to pat her back for a little while. Then she may get bored with this, decide just to stop going to bed, and want to go out and play. At this point, like most parents, you will usually have had enough. It all ends in tears and anguish and the whole process can take hours.

Keep in mind, too, that at this age your baby is becoming increasingly vocal. Her favourite word may well be 'No' but she will be communicating more and more with you through words. She can and will call out for you.

What your baby is doing with these behaviours is checking whether you have set limits on what she can and cannot do. She won't feel secure if she isn't certain about what's allowed. She feels better if things are predictable and occur in a set routine, and wants to know in advance in what order things take place. 'First Daddy reads me a story when I sit in his lap, then I kiss everyone good night. Then Mummy takes me into the bedroom, turns off the light and says "night night". Then she goes out of the room but leaves the door open.' A baby of this age (and older children, too) feels a sense of security from hearing her parents moving about outside and from other peaceful household noises, such as cleaning up the kitchen or Daddy's favourite CD, or Mummy tapping on the computer or talking on the telephone.

"A baby of this age feels secure if she can hear the regular sounds of life in the household going on around her as she is falling asleep."

17 month old wakes up for a long time in the middle of the night

My daughter has started waking up at night, at about 2 a.m., and staying awake for one, two, or even three hours. Usually she just wants to get up and play. What can be causing this? She rarely cries, except of course if she is awake alone for a long time. We took her to the doctor, but he said there was nothing wrong with her, which I wasn't really worried about anyway. But it's so strange, she has always slept well and we just don't understand what is going on. We have tried everything possible, like bringing her up into our bed, but then she just wants us to get up and play with her.

I don't know where this all comes from – nothing in her life has changed.

ARNA'S ANSWER

Your letter doesn't give me enough information to be able to tell what needs to be worked on. But the likely reason things have changed is that your daughter's sleep timings are not right or that they vary from day to day. You need to have fairly set sleep times. By that I mean when she wakes up in the morning, when she goes to sleep in the evening and when she naps during the day (you can use the illustration on page 126 as a guide). You need to keep this totally constant every single day – including weekends and holidays. The most common reason why a baby wakes for long periods during the night is a nap time that is too late in the day.

Follow-up letter

You know, that could be right, as she used to nap from 1 to 3:30 p.m. but it's been getting gradually later and later. I didn't know that it could be such an important issue. At night she sleeps from about 8 p.m. to 7 a.m. I'm going to try what you suggest.

18 month old wakes up earlier and earlier in the morning

Our problem isn't really big, but it's getting worse, so I decided to get in touch with you. Since our son started taking just one nap during the day, he has started to wake up earlier and earlier in the morning. He has always been a morning person, but 5 a.m. is a little too early. I'm just not ready to get up then. Before, he woke up at 6 or 7 a.m. and fell asleep at 8 in the evening. That worked well. He takes a nap at nursery from 11 a.m. to 2 p.m. His weekend schedule is the same. He is always fine with going to sleep in the evening – we put him in bed and he falls asleep peacefully. We've tried to push his bedtime later but it doesn't make any difference. I was wondering whether I ought to wake him up a bit earlier from his nap, say at 1 p.m. or so. What do you think about that? Can you make any suggestions, or is there nothing we can do? He has lots of energy during the day, so he clearly tolerates these timings just fine. Perhaps I just need to accept that things are like this.

Yours sincerely and in hopes of help for a father who would prefer not to have to wake up every morning at 5.

ARNA'S ANSWER

Some babies are morning people by nature. This is something that's often really hard to change, and parents sometimes just need to adapt and go to sleep earlier ourselves. But I want to ask you one thing. Could it be that he is nodding off for a few minutes in the late afternoon, between 4 and 6 p.m.?

Follow-up letter

You are right, he is. Sometimes he takes a quick snooze in the afternoon, when we go to eat at his grandparents' at the weekend, or when we pick up his mum from work. Could that be what's messing things up?

ARNA'S ANSWER

Yes, it could be the reason. Try to put a stop to these quick naps for two or three weeks, and see what kind of effect this has.

20 month old needs two hours to fall asleep and it's getting worse

Our daughter is quite determined but fun and cheerful. She is our first child and she bosses us around a lot. We are worried that she is not getting enough sleep. During the day she is more tired and irritable than she used to be. Until she got an ear infection four months ago, she had always slept well and fallen asleep on her own. Since then there is no end of trouble when she is supposed to go to bed. She is also so tired in the mornings that we have to wake her up. We've been advised to stop letting her take a nap, but I'm just not sure what she'd be like during the day then. She goes to bed at 8 p.m., and we were used to reading to her and kissing her good night before leaving the room.

Her daytime nap is 1½ hours long, after lunch, at nursery. She falls asleep straight away there, but at home at the weekend it's difficult. We're now driving her around for up to an hour until she falls asleep, because if she misses her nap at midday she falls asleep around 4 p.m. and gets very irritable during the evening. We have tried putting her down to sleep later in the evenings but that hasn't changed anything. Now we put her to bed at 8 p.m., and she immediately starts complaining. She wants to kiss Daddy good night again, she wants us to read more, she wants a different stuffed animal, she wants something to drink – always something new. She can't say very much in words, but it's amazing how well she can convey what she wants. When we say 'no' she goes totally out of control. We have tried to be strict, but she can cry for ages and we always give in before she does.

We can't keep on like this. Our daughter isn't as she ought to be. We've taken her to the doctor several times but they can't find anything wrong with her.

ARNA'S ANSWER

I totally agree with you that you shouldn't discontinue her naps. That would just make things worse. It's good that you are working to keep the timing of her naps consistent, even if you are having to use the car at the weekends. This is better than letting her sleep later in the day. Bear in mind that any sleep after 2 p.m. can disturb her night-time sleep.

Her ear infection set this chain in motion, but it is her desire for control that is keeping it going. Above all, she is testing out your limits. She is checking to see what she's allowed to do and decide. She is old enough that you unfortunately need to deal with this in a very determined way. You have to take the bedtime routine completely out of her control, because allowing her to have a say has brought things into complete chaos.

Change the routine: If possible, get someone else to take her for a single night. The idea here is to make a very clear and definite break in how things are done.

Change what you do for her before she goes to bed. Stop reading in the bedroom and read in the living room instead. Then it'll be clearer when reading time is over. Read outside the bedroom, let her kiss everyone good night, let her have a drink in the kitchen and then take her to her bedroom and lay her down to sleep. It's best if the parent who she obeys better takes care of this to start with, while the other parent leaves the house at least 15 minutes before bedtime. This reduces the chance that she'll cry for the other parent.

Alter your response: Next, sit by the door in the bedroom and act as if you neither hear nor see what she is doing or asking for, at least for a few minutes. Then you can respond to her calmly, saying 'We'll do that in the morning' or 'No, good night dear.' Speak in very short sentences and don't raise your voice. Be calm but determined. If she throws everything out of her cot, and she probably will, just let it all lie there for a few minutes. Don't put it all back in her cot immediately. You should, in short, respond to her only every few minutes and you shouldn't do or say too much: the less you can do, the better. If this takes one to two hours, which could easily happen with a very determined baby, stay consistent the whole time, except that you can lengthen the time that you wait between responses.

The main points are to stay with her, to be calm, and to do as little as possible. I know this doesn't sound like fun, but the current situation doesn't sound

much like fun either. Before taking such tough measures, however, have your baby checked over by her doctor. It would be very hard to wake up the morning after starting this new routine and find that your baby had a recurrence of her ear infection.

Follow-up letter

I wanted to let you know how things went. The first evening was horrible. She threw everything out of her cot except the mattress, and that only because she couldn't manage it. She needed two hours to fall asleep. Actually that's about the same amount of time she has needed recently, too. In any case, she did finally fall asleep. The next evening we went through the whole routine again. She didn't want to go to bed, but didn't complain as much – there were a few moments of spirited protest but nothing like the first night. Now five nights later it's only taking 5 to 10 minutes to get her to sleep, with no meltdowns. It's just unbelievable!

I wanted to ask you how long I should keep sitting in the doorway? I'm not against continuing, as long as it's not, like, for years.

ARNA'S ANSWER
Precisely, it's not good to keep up sitting in the doorway too long. It's best to do it for just four to six evenings, as otherwise she might start to try to get you to do all kinds of things for her. Make the change straight away, this evening. Usually starting to leave the room goes very easily. Follow the instructions on page 47.

♥ Special situations

Many situations can affect a child's sleep. Being born premature is one of them which, in addition to having an impact on a baby's sleep, can also affect how parents behave around their child. Having more than one small baby in a household can also affect how both babies sleep. Illness, too, is well known to disrupt a baby's sleep. Some babies undoubtedly sleep longer when they are sick, but more sleep poorly as pain or discomfort may make it difficult to fall asleep or can wake them up during the night.

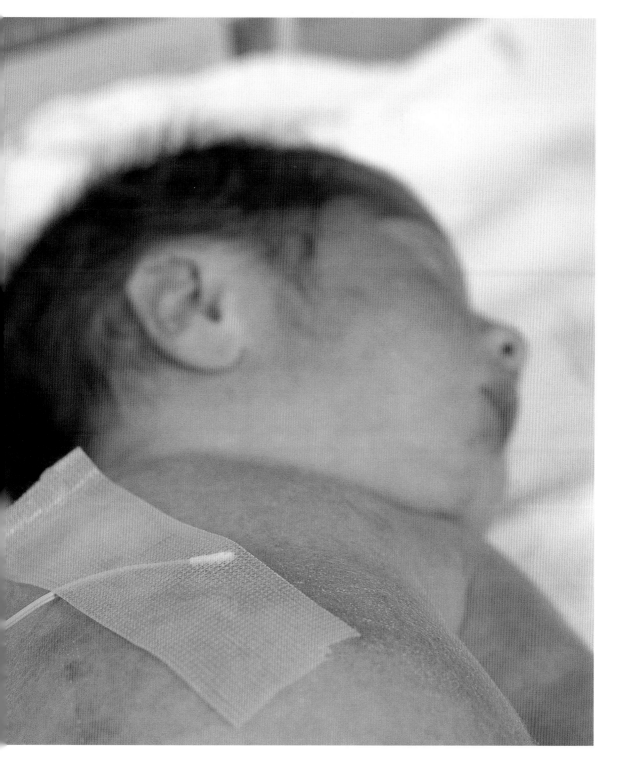

Premature babies

Parents of premature babies often wonder whether they sleep differently from full-term infants and whether there are any particular sleep-related issues that they need to consider. By 'premature' I mean a baby who is born before the 37th week of pregnancy. My discussion here applies to healthy premature babies. Premature babies often stay on the neonatal ward until around the time of their original due date. From then on their care is generally the same as that of other newborns. There are, however, a few points about premature babies, which are good to bear in mind.

COMING HOME

Parents naturally look forward to the day when their baby comes home, but this can also often cause a certain amount of anxiety. If your baby was premature, you should look at the first weeks at home as an adjustment period, both for you and your baby. It's best to keep this period very quiet and not try to do too much. If your baby has been in the special care baby unit (SCBU), you are probably used to

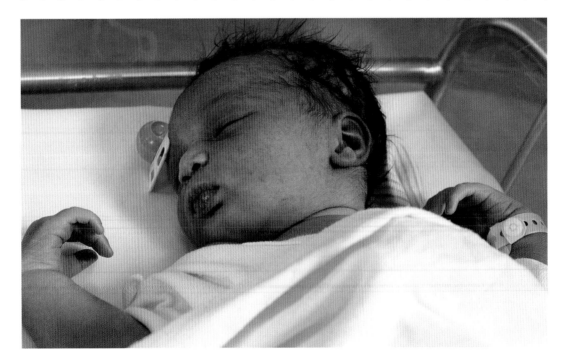

always having someone around to ask for help and advice. Don't feel you are on your own: it's always good to consult your doctor or health visitor if you are worried about your baby's wellbeing.

You may find it easier to make the transition from hospital to home if you keep to the hospital routines. In the SCBU perhaps his nappy was always changed before feeds, or after. Babies react in various ways when they are brought home. Some are completely at ease straight away, while others are upset by the change. If your baby is ill at ease after coming home, he should be given time to adjust to the different environment there. On the SCBU there is quite a bit more noise, light and traffic than at home. Many parents notice that their premature baby sleeps best when guests are present and people are talking. If that's the case with your baby, you can turn the radio on in his room and keep the lights on all night. Slowly you can wean your baby away from this, by dimming the lights and lowering the volume of the radio.

SLEEP NEEDS

Premature babies spend more time in light-sleep stages than full-term babies. Premature babies sometimes also murmur quite a bit during the light phases of their sleep. You should take care not to respond to this too quickly, as it is very easy to wake up a baby who is in this state. Usually you can base your expectations of your premature baby's sleep needs on his original due date. Thus, if your baby was born eight weeks premature, he should have similar sleep needs to a full-term baby who is two months younger. This, however, does vary from baby to baby. The main thing is for your baby to have a definite routine or rhythm to his sleeping times, rather than for him to sleep a certain number of hours or to take a particular number of naps.

Some babies who have been in the SCBU for a long time continue to wake up to feed every three hours – long after they would normally have stopped. When your baby weighs 3 kilos (6½ pounds), with his doctor's approval, you can work on lengthening his first stretch of sleep at night from three hours to four, and then to five and so on (see page 78). The main emphasis should be on lengthening one night-time sleep period, without any feeding. For your baby, the easiest approach is to lengthen the first sleep period.

Twins and close siblings

The care of twins or triplets always demands more planning than the care of a single baby and this applies particularly to sleep. In order to make your home life easier, try to get your babies to wake up at the same time in the morning and take their daytime naps at the same time. Consider, for example, eight-month-old twins, one of whom needs more sleep than the other. It's sensible to wake both of them at the same time in the morning – say 7 a.m. Both then have a nap at 9:30 a.m. and are allowed to sleep as long as they want. One wakes up at 11 a.m. and the other at 11:30. Both are then laid down for their second nap at 2 p.m. and again allowed to sleep as long as they wish. One wakes up at 3:30 p.m. and the other at 4 p.m. In this approach, the twin who sleeps more is woken up in the morning after the other wakes up on his own, but then is allowed to sleep longer during the day. This lets both babies get the sleep they need.

When dealing with twins where one (or both) has a sleep problem of some sort, it is usually easier to let them sleep in separate rooms some of the time for two reasons. The first is that if one twin starts to cry, the other can wake up. The other reason is that you will respond too quickly to a twin who wakes up (in order to avoid the other twin waking up) and in doing so, this twin will come to believe that this is a household with really good, quick night-time service.

You also need to keep in mind that there is often a lot of competition between twins and triplets for your attention. It's common for such babies to want to occupy the same spot in their parents' bed. This also happens with siblings who are close in age. If your younger child still sleeps in your room, your older child will frequently want to come into your bed. In this case, it's often more convenient to put your children in the same room, and it's likely that they will sleep better there since your older child won't need to worry whether his younger sibling is getting an 'unfair' share of your attention.

It's always advisable for the parents of multiples or children who are close in age to schedule special 'Daddy time' and 'Mummy time' for each child. This doesn't have to take a lot of time or have to be done every day. For example, take 20 minutes once a week to go outside and play or feed the ducks. With twins, one twin can sleep at his grandparents', or go on a short trip or on an outing with one parent. Everyone needs a chance to be alone with their parents sometimes, and to have a break from having to compete for attention with their siblings.

Illness and sleep

When babies are ill, it usually disturbs their sleep. A baby who is repeatedly ill should always see a doctor – it's better to go to the doctor too often than too seldom. Many babies sleep less well than usual when they are sick, and then start sleeping better again once they recover. Some babies, though, continue to sleep poorly after getting over an illness. These babies may need a little assistance in learning to sleep well again.

ILLNESS FOLLOWING A NEW SLEEP ROUTINE

A baby who has just become used to a new sleep routine and then is ill may want to 'regress' to his old ways during an illness. He may, for example, have adjusted to no longer feeding at night but will need to do so while he is sick. In this situation, you should avoid reintroducing an old routine as it may be difficult to regain the progress your baby had made. Instead, tend to your child differently. If he was used to having a bottle in your bed, don't let him do that again; let him drink from a cup while you hold him in your arms to comfort him. A baby who has just become used to sleeping to his own bed in his own room after a long time in his parents' bed shouldn't be brought back into your bed if he is ill. Instead, one of you should sleep on a mattress in your baby's room to give him the closeness he needs and monitor his condition while he is sick, without reintroducing a habit that he had grown out of.

GASTRIC REFLUX

If your baby vomits easily or suffers from gastric reflux, you should aim to stop night-time breastfeeding as soon as your baby is sufficiently mature. Drinking liquids at night can cause heartburn, and make babies wake up and cry. It is best to give your baby's tummy a complete rest during the night. How to reduce or stop night feeds is discussed in chapter 4 (pages 70–131). It is important for the baby to go to bed at a similar time each evening, and also to go to bed with a full tummy. That means feeding him well during the evening. When he is old enough (about six months), he

Teething and sleep

Teething pain is not inevitable and, even if your baby is affected, it may not disturb his sleep routine.

Baby paracetamol will reduce any pain, or try rubbing a topical analgesic on to your baby's gum before bed.

Offer a drink of cold water in a bottle or cup at bedtime to cool his gums.

General tips for babies with gastric reflux

There are several simple ways you can help a baby with gastric reflux to feel more comfortable:

✓ If your baby is newborn, it's good to let him lie on his right side for a little while when laying him down after a feed.

✓ As soon as your baby is sufficiently mature, cut out night-time feeds.

✓ Don't let your baby go to sleep straight after having something to eat or drink. Wait at least 20 to 30 minutes.

✓ After your baby has had something to drink let him sit in a fairly upright position – but not so upright that his head falls on to his chest and so he slouches down, as that will press anything he has just eaten upwards.

✓ As your baby gets older and starts to eat solid food more often, it's good to feed him solids before sleep (both before naps and before going to bed at night) and to breastfeed or bottlefeed him when he wakes up. Solid food doesn't come back up as easily as liquids.

should have some solid food an hour or so before going to bed. When he starts having solids three times a day, this should be once in the middle of the day and then twice in the evening, for example at 6 and 8 p.m. then he should be put to bed 30 to 60 minutes later. A baby with gastric reflux should not be given anything to drink in the minutes just before he goes to sleep. Always leave 20 to 30 minutes after a feed before putting your baby to bed.

EAR INFECTIONS

An ear infection makes it difficult for a baby to sleep. An infection doesn't usually disrupt a baby's ability to fall asleep on his own, but may disturb him soon after he falls asleep and when he moves around during the night. Your baby will feel pain and start to whimper. It can be difficult to judge whether such behaviour occurs because of discomfort in your baby's ears or not. To know for sure, you must consult a doctor. Babies who have had repeated ear infections can sometimes continue to complain at night even when nothing is really wrong any more. They are just stuck in a habit, which originally started because of their illness. The risk of this happening is higher if your baby is very active and determined.

Babies who are prone to ear infections or fluid in the ears should not breastfeed or bottlefeed while lying down; doing so carries a risk that milk will flow into the eustachian tube and add to the baby's discomfort. Babies who feel pain or discomfort in their ears often like to suck on something. If your baby is in pain, it's good to give him a dummy, both as a means of comfort and also a way of loosening the blockage in his ears.

ALLERGIES AND SLEEP

Statistics show that the number of babies and children with allergies and food intolerances is on the rise. Allergies can be difficult to detect since symptoms are wide ranging and include colic, upset tummy, rashes, asthma, eczema, breathing difficulties, hyperactivity, swelling of the throat and anaphylactic shock. The prevalence of allergic reactions is one of the main reasons to introduce solid foods one at a time and during the day so that you can spot a potential adverse reaction (see page 104).

In very young babies who have trouble sleeping, an allergic reaction to cow's milk may sometimes be put down to colic. If your baby is inconsolable for what seems like hours on end, and does not sleep, even when you know he is exhausted, see your doctor to rule out an allergy to cow's milk. If you are bottlefeeding, you may be advised to try a different type of formula. If you are breastfeeding, your own diet will need some modifications. Eliminating dairy products in the mother's diet means that she can't pass the offending dairy protein on to her baby through her breast milk.

Treating an ear infection

See your doctor who will decide whether your baby needs antibiotics.

Use over-the-counter medication to help to relieve the pain.

Try placing a warm water bottle or warm compress on the ear.

Pat or rub your baby's back or tummy to help soothe him to sleep.

"Always tailor your response to a baby's illness according to the severity of the condition."

Index

Figures in **bold** indicate Arna's answers to parents' letters.

Translation into English effected with a grant from

Bókmenntasjóður
The Icelandic Literature Fund

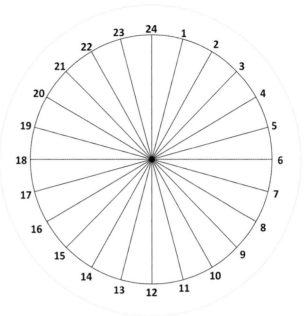

Acknowledgments

p3, p70 Laurence Monneret /
Getty Images; p98 Liz
Banfield / Getty Images;
p114 Brooke Fasani
Auchincloss / Corbis; p120
PhotoAlto / Sandro Di Carlo
Darsa / Getty Images; p124
Peter Reali / Corbis; p128
Plush Studios / Getty Images

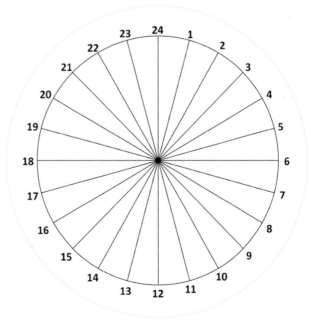

Also available from Carroll & Brown to help you look after your new baby

BABY MASSAGE
by Peter Walker

Knowing how to massage your baby is one of the most important skills a parent can learn. It will enable you to help your baby relax and cope better with stress, promote his or her development and improve muscular coordination and flexibility. Above all, it's fun for both parents and baby and will help strengthen the bond between you.

ISBN: 978 1 907952 03 6

A DAD'S GUIDE TO BABYCARE
by Colin Cooper

This comprehensive guide makes it easy for dads to take care of their infants – whether on a daily basis or only occasionally. It shows how to feed, change, dress, handle and amuse newborns to older toddlers and to handle tricky situations like bed times and illness. Filled with sage advice from a dad who has successfully raised his own children, it's invaluable for all fathers new to babycare.

ISBN: 978 1 904760 56 6

Sold in high street and online bookshops and at www.carrollandbrown.co.uk

Eloise
Undercover